WHEN LOVE IS *not* Perfect

by

MARIE SONTAG

Aglow.Publications

A Ministry of Women's Aglow Fellowship, Int'l.
P.O. Box 1548
Lynnwood, WA 98046-1558
USA

Cover design by David Marty

Unless otherwise noted, all scripture quotations in this publication are from the Holy Bible, New International Version. Copyright 1973, 1978, 1984, International Bible Society. Other versions are abbreviated as follows: KJV (King James Version), NASB (New American Standard Bible).

ISBN 0-932305-85-7

DEDICATION

To Grandma Caroline Arnold,
whose nurturing ways taught me much about God
during the short time I knew her.

Acknowledgements

Many thanks to those who shared their stories, as well as to my writing friends, Jane Baker, Gloria Chisholm, Audrey Dick, Pamela Erickson, Eileen Gunn, Marcy Lidtke, and Pauline Youd. Without their prayers, encouragement, and help, I could not have written this book.

Contents

PART VI
Shaking out the Welcome Mat

Introduction

Recovering from the effects of abuse is, at times, a lonely, painful process. Just when we need support and encouragement from God and others the most, we're the least inspired to seek it out. I have written *When Love Is Not Perfect* with this in mind. Each chapter contains discussion questions that will help clarify the main points in that particular segment of the book. To get the most out of this material, find a person or group with whom you can work through the questions. Each chapter also has a section, "God's Nurturing Words to You," containing paraphrases of Scripture relating to the specific issues in that chapter. Many who shared their stories here wished to remain anonymous, so most of the names have been changed.

"The deeper that sorrow carves into your being, the more joy you can contain."[1] Whether you are a victim of abuse or wish to gain insight into the nature and effects of abuse, I hope the examples and scriptural principles shared here will help transform the sorrow carved by abuse into a cavern of joy.

Part I

Surveying Damaged Foundations

1
...
What Is Abuse?

Responding to a report of a choking child, emergency medical personnel entered Joel Steinberg's Greenwich Village apartment. Inside they found the bruised, comatose body of his six-year-old adopted daughter, Lisa. She died four days later from injuries doctors likened to the impact of a fall from a three-story building.

A year after Lisa's death, Steinberg, who had illegally adopted her, stood trial for striking the blows that caused her death. What attracted millions to watch the televised testimony of Hedda Nussbaum, Steinberg's lover, as she unfolded to the jury her account of Lisa's beating? Why did so many feel outraged when the jury cleared Steinberg of murder charges and convicted him only of first-degree manslaughter?[1]

If statistics are correct, as many as one out of four adults who followed the Steinberg trial probably experienced some form of abuse as a child.[2] Many people identify with the misfortunes of others because, as psychiatrist Philip Kavanaugh, who practices in Los Gatos, California, states, they can vicariously relive their own pain and yet remain emotionally distant. Abused children usually bury their pain, but evidences of it creep into their adult life in subtle and, sometimes, not so subtle ways.

In my mid-thirties a doctor linked my chronic migraines and inexplicable joint pains to blocked memories of abuse I had experienced as a child. As memories of the abusive incidents surfaced, my non-Christian therapist explained my need to "re-parent" myself. As he explained the process, I knew the only one adequate to re-parent me was God. A study of the nurturing side of God's character played a key role in my recovery process.

Like many, I initially had no idea what constituted abuse, its prevalence, or its long-range effects. As I studied the subject, I learned that abuse falls into three categories: emotional, physical, and sexual. However, according to John Crewdson, author of *By Silence Betrayed*, defining abuse and keeping accurate records of it is more of an art than a science.[3]

EMOTIONAL ABUSE

The National Committee for Prevention of Child Abuse (NCPCA) defines emotional abuse as anything from neglect and rejection, to deliberate cruelty and humiliation.[4] The NCPCA believes the number of emotional abuse cases looms much larger than the 250,000 reported annually.

One of the reported cases of emotional abuse involved seven-year-old Russell Baptist. His mother, Mary Bergamasco, disciplining him for stealing some baseball cards, six dollars, a belt buckle, and another child's toy, tied him to a chair in their front yard. She drew on his face with a blue felt-tipped pen and fashioned a pig's snout from an egg carton and attached it to his nose. She then put a cardboard sign on his chest that read, "I'm a dumb pig. Ugly is what you will become every time you lie and steal. . . . My hands are tied because I cannot be trusted. This is a lesson to be learned. Look. Laugh. Thief. Stealing. Bad boy."[5]

The justice system in Alameda County, California, aware of the negative effects such abusive parenting could have on Russell, placed him and his one-year-old half-sister, Jennifer, in temporary foster custody until a trial to determine their permanent custody could be heard.

Bev's emotional abuse went unreported. No court system determined her need for "re-parenting." But her emotional life revealed the scars.

Bev's parents divorced when she was two. Her mother sent her to boarding school to complete both sixth and seventh grade. "I felt rejected, unloved, and unimportant," Bev shared, recalling her time away from home. "I cried almost every day that first year." While Bev adjusted to boarding school, her mother travelled around the world with a boyfriend. By the time she finished high school, Bev had lived with five different "fathers."

"I became a Christian when I was seventeen," Bev related. "I read Psalm 68:5, 'A father to the fatherless, a defender of widows, is God in his holy dwelling,' and clung fiercely to that promise. How I needed a father."

As Bev grew in her relationship with Christ, she learned that her heavenly Father would never reject her. "But that doesn't mean Satan, the father of lies, doesn't tempt me to think otherwise," she quickly added. "Sometimes I feel like God's withholding his love when I fail to pray consistently or spend time in the Word. That's when I need God's nurturing words the most—words like Hebrews 13:5, 'Never will I leave you; never will I forsake you.' "

PHYSICAL ABUSE

Physical abuse may seem more obvious than emotional abuse, but it too defies concise definition. The standard proof of physical abuse in criminal cases requires doctors to have "reasonable medical certainty" that physical abuse actually took place. The February 23, 1989, issue of *The New England Journal of Medicine* suggests a doctor diagnose an injury as physical abuse when the reason for it given by the child's caretaker fails to match the medical findings of the case. The *Journal* estimates that as many as 600,000 to two million children are physically abused each year. According to Sally Cooper, executive director of the National Assault Prevention Center, "Child abuse is the second leading cause of death for children under three in the nation."[6]

Perhaps the "pig" boy, Russell Baptist, should feel grateful that he was his mother's third child, and not her second. One night, Mary Bergamasco's second child, a three-month-old son, died after suffering a broken back and fractured skull. Her husband pleaded guilty to second-degree murder and served three years in jail.

"He broke my baby in two like a stick," Mary declared.[7]

Physical abuse can also occur within religious groups. On October 14, 1988, eight-year-old Dayna Broussard was beaten to death. She received the beating while in the care of the Ecclesia Athletic Association, an Oregon-based religious group founded by her father, Eldridge Broussard Jr., who also founded the Watts Christian Center in Los Angeles. Dayna died from multiple injuries to the head, chest, and limbs. Her body also evidenced scars, including whip marks, according to an Oregon state medical examiner.

The Oregon Children's Services Division immediately received custody of the group's fifty-three children, ranging in age from one-and-a-half months to sixteen years. Some of the youngsters had suffered as many as eight hundred systematic beatings with paddles, electrical cords, or other devices. The Clackamas County prosecutors said the children were forced to watch and count as others were beaten, including Dayna Broussard the night she died.[8]

Add fifty-three more to the number of children who need to experience God's re-parenting.

SEXUAL ABUSE

The National Center on Child Abuse and Neglect defines sexual abuse as "contacts or interactions between a child and an adult when the child is being used for the sexual stimulation of that adult or of another person."[9]

Margaret O. Hyde, author of *Sexual Abuse—Let's Talk About It*, broadens that definition. She states, "Sexual abuse may be committed by a person under the age of eighteen when that person is older than the victim or when the abuser is in a position of power or control over another child. The contact in sexual abuse may involve touching or it may be a nontouching offense."[10] Hyde also states that spying on a child while he undresses, suggesting that a child undress in front of an adult, or an adult exposing himself in front of children as in exhibitionism are all nontouching forms of sexual abuse. She also classifies obscene phone calls or communicating with children in some other way for immoral purposes as sexual abuse. "These kinds of abuse are less obvious than the touching kind," she writes, "but they, too, can hurt a child and leave long-lasting scars."[11]

17

When Love Is Not Perfect

According to a 1985 *Los Angeles Times* survey, as many as one out of four Americans may have been victims of sexual abuse. The *Times* telephoned 2,627 men and women from every state in the nation. Of those polled, 27 percent of the women and 16 percent of the men admitted they were sexually abused as children. One-third of the victims told no one about their abuse at the time, living with their secret well into adulthood.[12]

Such high statistics deserve closer attention, especially from the Christian community.

Dan grew up in a godly home. His grandfather served as a pastor, and both of his parents were active in their church. Because of Dan's strong Christian background, he had difficulty coming to grips with the suicidal thoughts he often entertained while attending a Christian college.

A psychology class assignment led Dan to interact with therapists working in a children's home for sexual abuse victims. As he observed the children, Dan found himself identifying with their behaviors and emotions. One day he mentioned the similarities to his school counselor as they met to discuss his suicidal feelings.

"That brought about a change of focus in my own personal therapy," Dan shared. "It was hard to accept, but I remembered my mother committing incest with me when I was a child."

In therapy, Dan recalled abusive acts perpetrated on him by more than nine different people, including relatives and teachers.

"Recovery can be frightening," Dan confessed. "What gets me through is knowing the Lord is with me, step by step," he explained. "Since my childhood abusers were trusted relatives and teachers, now, as an adult, I find it hard to trust anyone in authority. Because it's difficult for me to submit to authority figures, I change jobs often.

God's healing me, step by step, and I know he will eventually get me past this hurdle, too. I take it a day at a time."

Linda found no comfort among her church friends when she shared with them how the emotional, sexual, and physical abuse she experienced as a child had affected her adult life.

"My father was an alcoholic," she told me. "He hated for us kids to show any emotion and punished me when I cried. One day, when he saw tears in my eyes, he threw me across the room into a wall.

"Because of a birth defect," she continued, "I had several eye operations before I turned eight. The kids at school made fun of me because I wore glasses and a patch over one eye. My parents regularly reminded me of how much money I cost them."

Linda's abuse also included sexual molestation. "I hated it when my parents dropped me off at Uncle John's so they could go out and party," she related. "Until recently, I couldn't remember why I hated going to Uncle John's so much—but then it came back to me. He used to bounce me on his knee and have me 'ride a horse.' Then he'd put his hand in my pants and fondle me.

"I never drank," Linda said, "but I grew addicted to the masks of hiding behind my smiles, denying my emotional pain, and flitting from one project to another. After becoming a Christian, it was easy to bury myself in church activities. I had worn my masks for so long, I came to believe that they reflected the real me."

Fortunately, Linda has begun to experience God's reparenting. Unfortunately, she had to discover it outside her Christian church fellowship.

"The Lord got me into a Twelve-Step program for adult children of alcoholics," she explained. "The people there identified with my pain. I could talk to them about anything, and they still accepted me. I got in touch with feelings I didn't even know I had. I learned to turn my will and my life over to God in a new way. He gave me the hope that, as my heavenly Father, he could remove my masks and restore the real me."

Those like Russell, Bev, Dan, Linda, and the fifty-three children abused while under the care of a religious group need more than just a scriptural prescription such as, "God works all things together for good" or an admonition to "forget what lies behind." They need a fresh perspective of the nurturing side of God's character, mirrored in the lives of caring individuals.

The following chapters explore the symptoms of adults abused as children and provide a biblical framework to help victims experience God's re-parenting. You may or may not identify yourself as an adult abused as a child. But, abused or not, the following information will better equip you to grow in wholeness and in your ability to sensitively minister to others.

TIME TO CONSIDER

1. Can you recall experiencing any of the abuse mentioned in this chapter? If so, do you feel comfortable talking about it? Why or why not?

2. How do you feel when others share glimpses of their abused childhoods with you? How do you respond to them?

3. The Christian psychologist Dr. Kevin Leman states, "The little boy or girl you once were you still are."[13] Do you agree or disagree? Why?

4. Look up the following verses. How does a relation-

ship with God offer hope to adults abused as children? Isaiah 58:12; Psalm 139:11, 12; John 8:31, 32; 14:14-20.

5. A well-known evangelical pastor recently lamented the Christian community's "problem-centered" focus. "Just focus on Jesus and God's Word," he stated, "and the problems will take care of themselves." Do you agree or disagree with his statement? Why?

GOD'S NURTURING WORDS TO YOU

"I am your Sovereign Lord, who knows how to sustain my weary ones with a word. I will awaken you, morning by morning. I will awaken your ear to listen and heal your heart so you may receive all the nurturing comfort I long to give you.

"In ancient times I told my children, 'Look to the rock from which you were cut, and to the quarry from which you were hewn.' I wanted my people to remember that Abraham, their father, and Sarah, their mother, were one when I called them. They had no children, and yet I promised to bless them and make them many. Even though Abraham and Sarah took matters into their own hands and bore Ishmael, I remained faithful to them. Out of their barrenness I brought forth a nation.

"Now, my child, I ask you to look to the rock from which you were cut. The memories may be painful, but, as you look, I promise to be with you. Abraham and Sarah were my chosen ones, and yet they did not always walk in my ways. So, too, when your parents and caretakers failed to walk in my ways, it hurt you. As you uncover your wounds, I promise to comfort you—to sigh deeply with you—over all the pain you experienced as a child. I will look with compassion on all your ruins. I will make your deserts like Eden and your wastelands like the gardens of

21

When Love Is Not Perfect

the Lord. Joy and gladness will be found in you, thanksgiving and the sound of singing." (Paraphrased from Isaiah 50:4; 51:1-3.)

2
...

Characteristics of Adults Abused as Children

The Child Assault Prevention (CAP) project holds workshops for schoolchildren and teachers throughout the United States. They train people to recognize and effectively deal with potentially abusive situations. The workshops are not designed to elicit immediate reports of abuse. However, within one year, in just one public school district, CAP workshops led to the discovery of 184 cases of sexual abuse, 76 cases of physical abuse, and 7 cases of "life-threatening" situations. The incidents "included a child who was punished by being bound, gagged, and kept in a closet, another who was threatened with a gun, and a third who had knife wounds."[1]

Most of today's adults, however, were not equipped to handle abuse they experienced as children. Instead, like

Bev, Dan, and Linda, they were often taught to offer unquestioned obedience and were not allowed to talk back to adults. If children generalized such standards to encompass *all* situations with *all* authority figures, they had no way to protect themselves from victimization. Like the biblical character, Tamar, they also had little hope of ever restoring their damaged foundations—unless they learned how God could re-parent them.

TAMAR

Amnon's pre-meditated rape of his sister, Tamar, left her devastated. Unfortunately, Tamar had no idea how to let God re-parent her. Second Samuel 13 relates the story. Tamar received a message from her father, King David: her brother, Amnon, was sick and she must go and prepare food for him. She left immediately. Imagine the scene.

"Please make the bread in my sight," Amnon requested.

Tamar moved her bowl to the other end of the table near the mat where Amnon lay. Amnon studied her every move as she kneaded the dough and shaped the cakes.

After the cakes had baked, Tamar placed them before Amnon.

"Oh," Amnon groaned, holding his head. "I don't know if I even have the strength to eat. Perhaps if, yes, if everyone leaves, except my beloved sister, Tamar, I may recover enough to eat."

At his command, all the servants left the room. Lying on his bed, Amnon weakly stretched out his hand. Tamar quietly placed a tiny cake in it. Suddenly Amnon threw the cake aside and grabbed Tamar's arm, pulling her down on top of him.

"Don't, my brother!" Tamar tried to pry herself loose. "Such a thing should not be done in Israel! Just speak to the king," she pleaded. "I am sure he will allow you to marry me. But not this!"

Amnon muffled his sister's cries with kisses and then raped her.

When King David heard about the incident, he flew into a rage. But he did nothing.

Second Samuel 13:20 describes the lasting effect Amnon's incest had on Tamar: "And Tamar lived in her brother Absalom's house, a desolate woman." The Hebrew word for desolate means stunned, wasted, destroyed, to grow numb.

What a contrast this picture of desolation provides when compared with the meaning of Tamar's name. Tamar comes from the root used in the Hebrew word for palm tree. To the Israelites, the palm tree symbolized nourishment, refreshment, and celebration. Its shade and fruit provided relief and sustenance when the Hebrews journeyed through the wilderness (see Exodus 15:27). God commanded them to use palm branches when celebrating the Feast of Tabernacles as a reminder of their deliverance from Egypt (see Leviticus 23:40-44).

However, without re-parenting, Tamar would never live up to her name. King David failed to obey God's laws that commanded the exile of anyone who had sexual relations with a sister (see Leviticus 18:9, 29). Rather than turn to God for nurture and comfort in the wake of her father's failure to act on her behalf, Tamar remained desolate the rest of her life.

JOSEPH

Had Tamar examined the life of Joseph, perhaps she could have caught a glimpse of God's re-parenting and survived the effects of her abuse. Unlike Tamar, Joseph did not suffer from a lack of fatherly attention. In fact, he got too much attention. "Now Israel loved Joseph more than any of his other sons. . . . When his brothers saw that their father loved him more than any of them, they hated him and could not speak a kind word to him" (Gen. 37:3, 4).

Their hatred led them to plot his death. Throwing him into a waterless cistern, they anticipated the desert sun would cause his untimely death. Then, when a caravan passed by, his brothers changed their minds and sold him into slavery.

Joseph ended up in Egypt where the Pharaoh's wife falsely accused him of trying to seduce her. The Pharaoh threw Joseph in prison where he languished without hope of release until he interpreted the dream of the king's cupbearer. Joseph asked the cupbearer to remember him when he got out, but two years passed before the cupbearer mentioned Joseph's name to Pharaoh.

The abuse Joseph experienced could have caused him, like Tamar, to grow desolate. But instead of wasting away, his faith flourished. He named his first-born Manasseh and said, "It is because God has made me forget all my trouble and all my father's household" (Gen. 41:51). Somehow, God enabled Joseph to put the past behind him. He named his second son Ephraim and said, "It is because God has made me fruitful in the land of my suffering" (Gen. 41:52). Like a palm tree flourishing in a desert, God nourished and sustained Joseph in the midst of his troubles.

THE GOD OF THE WOMB

But what of the Tamars of today who wither away because of their damaged foundations? Like Joseph, they need to experience the re-parenting of God spoken of in Psalm 103:1-13: "Praise the Lord, O my soul. . . . He redeems my life from the pit and crowns me with love and compassion. . . . As a father has compassion on his children, so the Lord has compassion on those who fear him."

The Hebrew word used here for compassion is also the Hebrew word for womb—that place of nurture, protection, warmth, and initial growth.

Isaiah 51:3 also speaks to those who need God's re-parenting: "The Lord will surely comfort Zion and will look with compassion on all her ruins." The Hebrew word used here for comfort means to sigh, to breathe strongly. Imagine the God of the universe holding you in his arms as you tell him how devastated your childhood abuse made you feel. Lean on his breast and hear him sigh deeply as he grieves with you. Then feel his strong arms around you as he promises to nurture you with his womb-like compassion. Knowing the God of compassion, the God of the womb, and the God of comfort who sighs deeply with us in our pain can restore our shattered foundations. However, before examining more specific ways God can re-parent us, let's take a closer look at the effects abuse has on children.

EFFECTS OF ABUSE ON CHILDREN

Abuse inflicts wounds of confusion, fear, shame, false guilt, and anger.[2] If children cannot safely express these emotions, they repress them out of a need for self-protection. But the wounds do not heal. Effects of the abuse may surface in various ways, such as in speech or learning disabilities.

Before Dan worked through his abused childhood, he suffered from visual dyslexia. A college reading test revealed that he read at a fourth grade level. He scored high on auditory skills but showed no mental imagery capability. He also could not distinguish between certain colors such as shades of yellow and blue.

After Dan began to experience God's re-parenting, his reading level gradually increased. When he remembered he was molested in a blue building, he began to distinguish shades of blue once again.

According to the Children's Self-Help Project, sponsored by the Stanislaus County Department of Mental Health, abused children may exhibit fear when visiting previously enjoyed places or people, or a fear of men or women in general. They may masturbate frequently or regress to bed-wetting and thumb-sucking. Some abused children seem to retreat into a fantasy world.[3] Others' academic performances dramatically change because of low concentration, frequent absenteeism from school, or behavioral problems in the classroom.[4] Effects of child abuse could show up in a loss of appetite, overeating,[5] or chronic insomnia.[6] Abused children may internalize their fear and anger over the abuse by repressing any conscious memory of it, or memories of the abuse could haunt them in night-terrors. Other symptoms of abuse may be self-mutilation and suicidal thoughts or talk, "picking at skin or scabs until they bleed, hitting self, cutting self, slapping self . . . sore throats, stomach aches, gagging, asthma, [or] upper respiratory disorders."[7] A few develop multiple personalities as a way of distancing themselves from the memories of their abuse.[8]

EFFECTS OF ABUSE ON ADULTS

When the festering wounds of abuse are carried into adulthood, they can result in an inability to develop intimate, trusting relationships.[9] In the first chapter, Dan spoke of his inability to trust employers. Adults abused as children often exhibit low self-esteem and a lack of self-identity.[10] Many have difficulty in feeling or expressing emotions.[11] Some try to compensate for a low sense of worth by over-achieving. Others develop compulsive or addictive behaviors to numb their unpleasant feelings.[12]

Abused adults may become "controllers," desperately trying to control everyone and everything around them.[13] Some, as Dan did, turn their anger inward and feel suicidal.[14] Many relate to others by taking on the role of a rescuer or caretaker.[15]

Adults abused as children often repeat their victimization by abusing their spouse or children. In a survey conducted at Abused Women's Aid In Crisis, Inc., out of fifty cases randomly selected from one thousand cases, eighty-one percent of the physically abusive partners "came from homes in which they themselves were beaten or where they had witnessed their own father abusing their mother."[16] And, according to Margaret Hyde, author of *Sexual Abuse—Let's Talk About It*, "As many as 81 percent of convicted child molesters are reported to have been molested themselves as children."[17]

As adults, victims of abuse may suffer inexplicable physical pain.[18] An abused childhood may also contribute to promiscuity or frigidity as a teen or as an adult.[19] Although these lists do not evidence abuse in every case, most survivors of abuse experience one or more of these symptoms at some point in their lives.

LEARNING TO DANCE AGAIN

As a young girl, I loved listening to music, singing, and dancing. When I was five, my mother enrolled me in dance lessons. But after four months of tap and ballet, I threw away my shoes. Later, when my mother insisted we deliver a Christmas present to my former dance teacher, I refused to get out of the car.

Until recently, I couldn't remember what made me so afraid to face my dance teacher again that Christmas. And I could never recall why I quit my lessons.

After the birth of my second child, I experienced chronic

pain in my hands, back, and ankles. Doctors ruled out arthritis, and finally settled on a diagnosis of fibrositis. But just as they couldn't give me a reason for its onset, they also couldn't find a cure. Having already suffered from migraine headaches for twelve years, I resigned myself to living with the pain—until a friend and therapist suggested an alternate diagnosis.

"Were you ever abused as a child?" she asked.

"Not me," I told my friend. A year earlier, my younger sister had confided in me; she had been sexually molested as a child. And yet I felt certain nothing had ever happened to me. Then God melted my defenses.

I remembered two incidents of molestation by close relatives; one occurred at the age of five and one when I was nine. But remembering didn't alleviate my physical pain. Drained of all energy, I took afternoon naps daily. If a door slammed while I slept, I'd wake up in a cold, panic-stricken sweat.

"What scares me about doors slamming?" I asked the Lord one afternoon. My body froze as the answer came. I remembered a basement door slamming shut.

During a session with a professional counselor I recalled my childhood fear of being left alone with my dance teacher in her basement for our weekly private lessons. I could hear the basement door shut and remembered a window high above my head. Now, with my counselor, I cried out in a child-like voice, "It's too high. I can't reach it."

Paralyzing fear gripped me. I sobbed uncontrollably, causing me to hyperventilate. But I couldn't remember what had frightened me so much.

Later that night I asked God to let me remember the incident when he knew I could handle it. A few days later I saw myself alone with my teacher in her basement. She exposed herself to me and when I cried out for help, she choked me and told me to shut up. When I kept crying, she repeatedly banged the right side of my head against the basement's cement block wall—the side where my migraines occur.

Then she threatened, "If you ever tell anyone about this, I'll kill you." I was only five at the time, and I believed her. I interpreted her threat to mean I couldn't even tell myself.

Remembering that incident helped me get in touch with a part of me I had buried. Slowly, I learned how to let God nurture and comfort the little girl inside who had locked the traumatic memories within her.

As God restores my damaged foundations, I find myself dancing once again—not physically, but emotionally. A few days after I remembered the abusive incident, I bought some donuts and actually carried on a conversation with the salesperson. I never would have done that before. A few weeks later, while driving to a luncheon appointment with Mary, my Bible study teacher, I felt my muscles tighten and sensed a headache coming on. I had unconsciously transferred the fear of my dance teacher to all strangers and authority figures, contributing to my migraines and fibrositis syndrome. When I simply told myself, "Mary's not going to kill me," the tenseness dissolved. As God re-parents me, I'm learning to relax and enjoy being me.

STORING UP THE TRUTH

Abuse survivors unconsciously develop survival techniques to help them cope with abuse and to protect themselves from further incidents. In the Afterword to the American Edition of *Thou Shalt Not Be Aware*, Alice Miller writes,

The truth about our childhood is stored up in our body, and although we can repress it, we can never alter it. Our intellect can be deceived, our feelings manipulated, our perceptions confused, and our body tricked with medication. But someday the body will present its bill, for it is as incorruptible as a child who, still whole in spirit, will accept no compromises or excuses, and it will not stop tormenting us until we stop evading the truth.[20]

Jesus said, "You will know the truth, and the truth will set you free" (John 8:32). As we pursue truth, God promises to bring hidden things into the light. Although the process may seem frightening, the rewards of wholeness are worth it.

Pastor and counselor David Seamands encourages us in *Putting Away Childish Things*,

Look back to find out where you are still allowing the inner child of your past to dominate your life, in order that you may become more responsible. Look back to discover where you need to change, where you need to forgive and be forgiven, where you need to be healed, and where you need to daily discipline yourself. Look back so that you may be yourself as you really were intended to be—a child of God set free by the healing power of the Holy Spirit.[21]

TIME TO CONSIDER

1. Summarize the different reactions Tamar and Joseph had to the abusive incidents in their lives.

2. Look over the effects of abuse on children and adults listed in this chapter. Are you aware of experiencing any

of these symptoms as a child or now as an adult? If so, which ones?

3. In what ways do you think abused children's defense mechanisms help them cope with abusive memories?

4. How does 1 Corinthians 13:11 relate to self-protection devices you may have used as a child?

5. According to Ephesians 3:16, where do we get the power to strengthen our inner being?

6. David Seamands suggests that shedding our childhood defense mechanisms and healing our inner child will take discipline. Some psychologists label the goal of this process "self-actualization" or finding our "higher self." But according to 1 Timothy 4:7, why do we seek God's re-parenting?

7. What does 1 Timothy 4:8 list as the benefits of this process?

8. Read 1 Timothy 6:6. If we are truly moving toward the goal of godliness, what else will we gain?

GOD'S NURTURING WORDS TO YOU

"My child, as you allow me to re-parent you, at times you may want to cry out as Job did: 'When I hoped for good, evil came; when I looked for light, then came darkness. The churning inside me never stops; days of suffering confront me.' Like David, at times you may feel overwhelmed by darkness. Even the light around you may seem like night.

"But know this: Even the darkness is not dark to me.

33

When Love Is Not Perfect

The night is as bright as the day. Darkness and light are alike to me. I know all you have gone through. I did not cause it. But because you live in a sinful world and I gave man free choice, this evil happened to you even though I love you very much. As Joseph experienced, I will bring good out of evil, if you let me. I have hemmed you in—behind and before; I have laid my hand upon you. Rest in my love.

"Believe in my light, even when all you see is darkness. Do not turn away from me in bitterness, wasting away as Tamar did. Remember, no matter how deep your pit, my love is deeper still. Hold on to my promises. I will redeem your life from the pit and crown you with love and compassion—my nurturing, life-sustaining, 'womb' compassion. I will satisfy your desires with good things so that your youth, even though damaged by the evil inflicted upon you, will be renewed like the eagle's, causing you to soar once again." (Paraphrased from Job 30:26-28; Psalm 139:11, 12, 4, 5; 103:4, 5.)

Part II

Laying a New Foundation

3

...

Dysfunctional Blueprint Versus God's Blueprint

My stomach churned as I read the front page news. The innocent, sweet face of a three-year-old girl stared up at me from a photo. The surrounding black and white newsprint detailed the murderous rampage she had survived, leaving seven people dead. The victims included the girl's mother and two sisters. The three-year-old had identified her father as the one who had slit her throat, as well as the throats of her two sisters, and then thrown them over an embankment next to a garbage dump. Somehow the girl had survived the night and was found the next morning.[1]

Such news sickens us. Parents have a God-given responsibility to care for their children. Most abuse is not as obvious as this. Yet any failure to follow God's blueprint for family life leaves cracks in a child's foundation for healthy living. Because of our sin nature, to some degree, we all experience the effects of growing up in dysfunctional families. The impact of those dysfunctions upon our lives and the lives of our children, however, depends upon our current desire to follow God's blueprint.

DYSFUNCTIONAL BLUEPRINTS

Simply defined, a dysfunctional family is one that doesn't function properly. Therapist Robin Norwood defines a dysfunctional home as one "in which your emotional needs were not met. . . . 'Emotional needs' does not refer only to your needs for love and affection. . . . even more critical is the fact that your perceptions and feelings were largely ignored or denied rather than accepted and validated."[2]

Eileen grew up in such a home. She recalls her father committing incest with her when she was five years old and her brother sexually abusing her when she was nine. Outwardly, her family appeared stable and well-adjusted. They attended church regularly, she never saw her parents argue, and, although not wealthy, the family always seemed to have enough money to meet their material needs.

"When I began to learn how God could re-parent me," Eileen shared, "I saw how far my family had deviated from God's blueprint and how it had affected our relationships. Mom grew up with an alcoholic father. She, in turn, became a workaholic, working many hours outside the home while Dad cared for us. A subtle 'family secret' promoted by Mom, which I think contributed to the incest, was that Dad really couldn't provide financially for us. I think it boosted her self-esteem to let us know she earned more money than Dad. She subtly gave us the message that we shouldn't let other people know, especially Dad, that *we* knew she could provide for us better than he could. Outwardly she wanted us to respect Dad, but in actuality we were to depend upon her to meet our needs."

Ill-equipped to follow God's blueprint, Eileen's family suffered the consequences of a dysfunctional family. Her parents' role reversal contributed to the emotional distance between the two of them. Unable to meet each others' needs, her parents looked to their children to meet their needs. Eileen's sister, also sexually abused by her brother, married an emotionally abusive man. Eileen's brother became a drug addict.

People growing up in dysfunctional families learn to accept their pattern of relating to one another as normal. As Eileen's family experienced, without God's re-parenting, it's difficult to break out of these harmful patterns and discover his blueprint.

TIES THAT BIND—FEATURES OF DYSFUNCTIONAL FAMILIES

Restrictive Rules

Many people accept their dysfunctional family life as normal because it's all they've ever known. Dysfunctional families often set up rules by which everyone must abide. These subtle rules can include not going outside of the family to get needs met, not expressing feelings openly, communicating wants and needs with one another indirectly through non-verbal messages, or using someone to act as a go-between. These families may avoid personal conflict through denial or their refusal to discuss problems. They set up unrealistic expectations of perfection and allow no change in the status quo. Those who "play" rather than work are made to feel guilty.

Repressive Roles

Restrictive rules of communication cast family members into repressive roles that keep the family functioning.

When Love Is Not Perfect

John Bradshaw, a counselor, speaker, and writer, explains, "In every case the person playing the role gives up his own unique self-hood. In dysfunctional families, the individual exists to keep the system in balance."[3]

In Eileen's family, she took on the role of caretaker, hero, and chameleon. She based her self-worth on how well she thought she met the needs of others in the family. Her childhood dreams included imagining herself as a hero—a sheriff who rounded up the "bad guys" or as Robin Hood routing the evil forces of Prince John.

Eileen's sister took on a "computer" role. She coped with her family's dysfunction by disassociating herself from her feelings. Many viewed her as calm and cool when, in reality, she felt very alone and too scared to feel.

Eileen's abusive older brother played the role of scapegoat. The family always identified him as the problem child. Eileen's younger brother filled the role of mascot or clown. He seemed to feel responsible for making everyone happy. When the family atmosphere grew tense, his humor usually smoothed things over. This family saw no problems in the way they related to one another.

(For a more thorough discussion of family rules and roles, see Virginia Satir's *Peoplemaking* or John Bradshaw's *On The Family*.)

The Fantasy Bond

Another reason people may unquestionably accept their abusive backgrounds as normal stems from a child's need to see his caretakers as capable and good. Admitting flaws in his parents is too frightening for a child. Without his parents, he would have no one to take care of him. Instead of seeing his parents as responsible for the abuse, he blames himself. Often children refuse to testify in court against their abusive parents because they reason they deserved whatever happened.

In *Dangerous Secrets*, Michael Weissberg shares an illustration of a fantasy bond carried into adulthood. A woman was overheard at a dinner party to say, "I am very close to my family. Growing up, they were always demonstrative and loving. When I disagreed with my mother, she threw whatever was nearest at hand at me. Once it happened to be a knife, and I needed ten stitches in my leg. A few years later, my father tried to choke me when I began dating a boy he didn't like. They are very concerned about me."[4]

Needy Parents

The most common element in abusive families is needy parents trying to get their needs met through their children. The children, given "adult" responsibilities, feel inadequate because they never *will* be able to meet their parents' needs; they feel abandoned because no one was ever there to meet their valid needs.

A significant part in Eileen's recovery from the effects of her childhood abuse occurred when her therapist asked Eileen to picture herself as a little girl. "Now imagine your parents coming into the room," he instructed. "What do you feel?"

Eileen remained quiet for a moment and then began to sob. "I feel like they're trying to take something from me that I'm not able to give them."

Later, as Eileen grew in her re-parenting process, she put more of the pieces together. "I see now that my parents were needy people. They didn't know how to let God meet their needs or how to really meet each other's needs. Instead they turned to us children for fulfillment. Ephesians 5:29 says a husband should nourish and cherish his wife. Mom got her nourishing and cherishing from us because we looked to her as our provider, rather than to Dad. Since

41

Mom was always working, Dad took from us sexually to relieve some of his frustrated need for intimacy. And since my older brother couldn't really look to Mom and Dad for the fulfillment of his emotional needs, he tried to wrench it from my sister through acts of sexual abuse."

GOD'S BLUEPRINT

God's blueprint for family life lays a foundation that instills love, competence, and worth in the family members. Ephesians 5:22-6:4 drafts the dimensions of God's blueprint for the family. Mom and Dad give to each other as God nurtures them. Husbands, as servant-leaders, love their wives as Christ loved the church and gave himself up for her. Wives subject themselves to their husband's leadership, just as the church subjects itself to Christ. Children obey and honor their parents. Fathers, who provide children with their first impression of God, do not provoke their children to anger, but bring them up in the nurture and admonition of the Lord. A sketch of a healthy family blueprint might look something like this.

First Timothy 5:8 instructs, "If anyone does not provide for his relatives, and especially for his immediate family, he has denied the faith and is worse than an unbeliever." Of course, parents can never meet *all* their children's needs. Healthy parents realistically face their inadequacies and look to God to fill in the gap. Second Corinthians 3:5, 6 clarifies the focus. "Not that we are competent to claim anything for ourselves, but our competency comes from God."

To follow God's blueprint, parents must avoid the temptation to use their children to meet their needs, but allow God to meet their needs and to re-parent them. Parents can then point to the Lord as the one who is all-sufficient to meet their children's needs as well.

Dysfunctional Blueprint Versus God's Blueprint

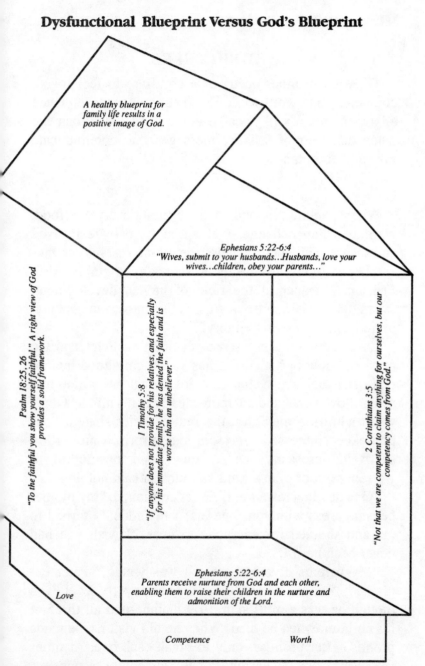

A healthy blueprint for family life results in a positive image of God.

Ephesians 5:22-6:4
"Wives, submit to your husbands...Husbands, love your wives...children, obey your parents..."

Psalm 18:25, 26
"To the faithful you show yourself faithful." A right view of God provides a solid framework.

1 Timothy 5:8
"If anyone does not provide for his relatives, and especially for his immediate family, he has denied the faith and is worse than an unbeliever."

2 Corinthians 3:5
"Not that we are competent to claim anything for ourselves, but our competency comes from God."

Ephesians 5:22-6:4
Parents receive nurture from God and each other, enabling them to raise their children in the nurture and admonition of the Lord.

Love

Competence

Worth

Parents need to lay a firm foundation of love, competence and worth, which enables the family to build their lives on a healthy basis.

THE BIG THREE

Three basic inner needs of a child are to feel loved, competent, and worthwhile.[5] Studies show that even when all of an infant's physical needs are met, they can die when deprived of sensory messages that communicate love and acceptance.[6]

Love

When parents respond to their infant's cry for food, warmth, a diaper change, or attention, the baby feels loved and secure. This security helps the infant trust his caretakers because his environment seems predictable. Erik Erikson, a leader in the field of human development, states that a basic sense of trust is the "most fundamental prerequisite of mental vitality."[7]

Love communicates a sense of belonging. Peter, a gifted musician now in his fifties, has vague childhood memories of sexual abuse. Incidents of verbal and emotional abuse, however, stand out more clearly in his mind. "Once, when admiring music on the radio," Peter shared, "our housekeeper crossed the room and surprised me with a sharp slap across my face. Although I had done nothing to warrant reproof of any kind, my mother said nothing.

"One day in a restaurant," Peter continued, "my mother became cross with someone else and suddenly turned to me and shouted for everyone to hear, 'I wish you had never been born.'

"My parents divorced when I was young," Peter explained, "and my father let me live at poverty level even though he was a millionaire. He disinherited all three of his children when he died. When he did visit us, he made promise after promise, only to break each one. At times God seems like my earthly father—distant, unresponsive, and given to exaggeration. I learned early in my Christian life to believe the facts, even when my feelings seem to contradict them."

In contrast to the inconsistent love we may have experienced as children, God's love will not disappoint us. It remains steadfast and unfailing in spite of our failures. Romans 5:5-8 says, "And hope does not disappoint us, because God has poured out his love into our hearts by the Holy Spirit, whom he has given us. You see, at just the right time, when we were still powerless, Christ died for the ungodly. Very rarely will anyone die for a righteous man, though for a good man someone might possibly dare to die. But God demonstrates his own love for us in this: While we were still sinners, Christ died for us."

Competence

Judges 6 showcases a man whose upbringing neglected to provide him with a solid foundation for living, especially in the area of competence. When God told Gideon to save Israel from the hand of the Midianites, Gideon replied, " 'But Lord . . . how can I save Israel? My clan is the weakest in Manasseh, and I am the least in my family.'

"The Lord answered, 'I will be with you, and you will strike down the Midianites as if they were but one man.'

"Gideon replied, 'If now I have found favor in your eyes, give me a sign that it is really you talking to me. Please do not go away until I come back and bring my offering and set it before you.'

"And the Lord said, 'I will wait until you return' " (Judg. 6:14-18).

Gideon grew up believing he came from the weakest clan in his tribe and that he was the least in his family. His feelings of incompetence made it difficult for him to trust God. "How can I know it's really *you* talking to me?"

When Love Is Not Perfect

Gideon asked God. The Lord, aware of Gideon's need for a new foundation, gently showed himself as trustworthy. "I will wait until you return," the Lord promised. When Gideon returned later with a young goat and some flour, he found the Lord still there. God touched the meat and bread Gideon had prepared, causing fire to consume them. Noticing the look of horror on Gideon's face, the Lord assured him, " 'Peace! Do not be afraid. You are not going to die' " (Judg. 6:23).

The next verse reveals Gideon's new perception of God. "So Gideon built an altar to the Lord there and called it 'The Lord is Peace' " (Judg. 6:24). The Hebrew translation for "The Lord is Peace" is *Yahweh-Shalom*. According to the Greek scholar Spiros Zodhiates, *shalom* means health, security, tranquility, welfare, success, peace, salvation, and wholeness.[8] In a short time, Gideon's personal insecurities and faulty image of God as powerless, uncaring, and one who had abandoned him and his people had changed into an image of an all-sufficient God who could use him to help restore peace and welfare to the nation.

Because of the trauma surrounding my physical and sexual abuse, I learned to fear the feeling of fear. Often this has prevented me from stepping out of my circle of confidence to try new things. Writing a book on abuse definitely qualifies as something outside my circle of confidence. When fears of incompetence plague me, I open my Bible to 2 Corinthians 3:5, 6. "Not that we are competent in ourselves to claim anything for ourselves, but our competence comes from God. He has made us competent as ministers of a new covenant—not of the letter but of the Spirit; for the letter kills, but the Spirit gives life." He has promised to give me the competence to do whatever he calls me to do.

Worth

A child who feels loved and competent develops a healthy view of his self-worth. Abusive homes, however, rarely supply a child with the building blocks needed to develop a healthy sense of worth. When this happens, psychologist Erik Erikson explains, the child often "accepts work as the only criterion of worthwhileness, sacrificing imagination and playfulness too readily."[9] This may account for the large number of workaholics who come from alcoholic homes.

Actress Susan Sullivan described the effects of her father's drinking on her school-age years. "Because of my father's drinking, my mother had to go to work. I was almost 10, and I became the little housekeeper, cleaning the kitchen, taking care of the house. . . . I never felt I was good enough, no matter what I did."[10]

In contrast, building our lives upon God's foundation instills a positive sense of worth. Ephesians 2:10 says, "For we are God's workmanship, created in Christ Jesus to do good works, which God prepared in advance for us to do." God has significant work for us to accomplish. Our worth in his sight, however, is not based upon how well we perform. He chose us before the creation of the world to be holy and blameless in his sight just because he loves us.

One summer at a Christian family camp I saw a wonderful example of a mother tuned in to her child's need for love, competence, and worth. As my one-year-old and I dangled our legs over the edge of the wading pool, a boy playing in the water with plastic measuring cups caught my attention. A little girl came over and asked the boy if she could play with one of his cups. He eyed his toys and then glanced up at his mother.

"No," the boy decided, looking back at the girl.

Immediately the little brunette squeezed her eyes shut

and beat the water with her fists.

The boy's mother, bewildered by the scene, gently tried to reason with her son. "Justin, are you sure you don't want to share one of your cups? You have three of them."

Justin clutched his cups, shook his head, and repeated, "No."

His dilemma touched both of us as we watched the tears stream down his face. She reached her arms out and hugged him tightly. "It's hard to share, isn't it?" She rocked him on her lap. Then turning to the girl she added, "Those are Justin's special cups. If you wait a little while, he may want to share them later."

When the mother's eyes met mine I smiled, recognizing the wisdom of her decision. Earlier in the week we had listened to Christian psychologist Dr. Bruce Narramore speak about the toddler's need for autonomy, which builds his sense of competence. Rather than shame Justin into sharing or force him to ignore his emotions, his mother identified with him. She recognized that keeping his cups at that point provided him with a necessary sense of individuality. She affirmed his uniqueness and worth: "Those are Justin's special cups." Hoping she had correctly tuned into his inner needs, she anticipated a positive change in his behavior: "Perhaps he'll want to share them with you later."

A NEW FOUNDATION

Without such re-parenting, those with unmet needs for love, competence, and worth build their lives upon faulty foundations. Jesus describes how, no matter what our background, we can build our lives upon a solid foundation.

"Therefore everyone who hears these words of mine and puts them into practice is like a wise man who built his house on the rock. The rain came down, the streams rose, and the winds blew and beat against that house; yet it did not fall, because it had its foundation on the rock. But everyone who hears these words of mine and does not put them into practice is like a foolish man who built his house on sand" (Matt. 7:24-26).

Gideon heard what God wanted to do through him, but because his need for love, competence, and worth had gone unmet, and because of the blurred image of God passed down to him from previous generations, he almost failed to act.

The abused can come to the Lord and gain a renewed understanding of who he is and of who they are—if they are willing not only to listen to his words, but to act on them as well. In the next chapter we will explore ways we can act on God's Word and so build our lives upon his solid foundation.

TIME TO CONSIDER

1. List the unhealthy rules and roles mentioned in this chapter. Did you experience any of these growing up? How have they programmed your adult life?

2. Can you think of at least two childhood incidents where your need for love, competence, and worth were met? How did they affect your self-esteem?

3. Think of at least two childhood incidents where a need for love, competence, or worth was not met. Have you carried scars? What are you doing about them?

4. In what ways can a lack of love, competence, or worth affect a person's image of God and his ability to serve him?

5. Look up Romans 5:5-8; 2 Corinthians 3:5, 6; Ephesians 1:4; 2:10. How can God's re-parenting provide us with a positive sense of love, competence, and worth?

GOD'S NURTURING WORDS TO YOU

"I have chosen you—I, who formed you in the womb. I will help you. Do not be afraid. Just as I pour water on thirsty land and streams on the dry ground, so I will pour out my Spirit on you. I love you with an everlasting, unfailing love. I will draw you to myself with loving-kindness. I will build you up again.

"You may have been hurt in the past and closed off doors of your life to the healing power of my Spirit. But, if you let me, I will go before you to level the mountains, to break down gates of bronze, and to cut through bars of iron. I will give you the treasures of darkness and riches stored in secret places so that you may know that I am the Lord.

"As you explore those secret places of hurt, I will be your refuge and your strength. I am an ever-present help in trouble. Do not fear, even if it seems as if the earth is giving way beneath you. Be still, and know that I am God. I will be your fortress of protection. I will tend to you like a shepherd. Feel my arms around you as I gather you in close to my heart. I will never leave you or forsake you. You will be able to say with confidence 'The Lord is my helper; I will not be afraid. What can man do to me?' " (Paraphrased from Isaiah 44:1-3; Jeremiah 31:3, 4; Isaiah 45:1-3; Psalm 46:1, 2, 10, 11; Isaiah 40:11; Hebrews 13:5, 6.)

4
...
Breaking New Ground

Adults abused as children must break new ground in their lives if they wish to implement God's blueprint. Not knowing another blueprint for family life exists, however, keeps many abuse survivors from laying down God's new foundation.

Such was the case for Sharon, a display designer, who grew up in a non-Christian home estranged from her father. She didn't know of another blueprint for family life until, at age twenty-six, she saw the James Dobson film series, "Turn Your Heart Toward Home." Within the first few minutes of the first film, Sharon began to cry. "Dr. Dobson explained that God planned for children to have two parents who would represent God to them, and he gave specific guidelines to follow on becoming godly parents. I realized I never had parents like that. I had no idea what it meant to have God as a Father who would love me, discipline me, and always be there. One thing I appreciate about God's Word is that it gives me those guidelines for living. I never had God's perspective on life while growing up."

IDENTIFYING COPING MECHANISMS

In addition to the lack of healthy role models, survivors of abuse may experience difficulty breaking new ground in their lives because of coping mechanisms they have developed in order to survive the trauma of abuse. These self-protection devices, often helpful to abuse victims in childhood, when carried into adulthood hinder a person's ability to fully implement God's blueprint.

Survivors employ two common coping mechanisms: they ignore their emotions and feel overly responsible for the wants and needs of others.

Susan, now an elementary school teacher, learned to ignore her emotions early in life. At age five, she told her mother her older brother had touched her private parts, and her mother made light of it. She received the same response every time she tried to bring up the subject and finally stopped talking about it. She decided her mother must know best, so she tried to ignore the uncomfortable feelings when her brother touched her. Instead, she developed a coping mechanism: numbing her emotions.

At twenty-one, Susan married a man who emotionally abused her. She endured his ill-treatment for several years, reasoning it was her Christian duty. Her childhood abuse had left her feeling so worthless and ashamed she thought she deserved to live with an abusive husband. Susan also felt a measure of worth because her husband needed her to take care of him. She worked full-time to help put him through school. When he spent money compulsively on such things as clothes or long-distance pornographic phone services, Susan put in more hours at work to cover the bills or went without food to ensure that her husband had enough to eat.

In *Women Who Love Too Much*, Robin Norwood explains that when people grow up ignoring their emotions, they lose touch with their feelings and are unable to make wise decisions about important aspects of their lives. "We often do not really know who we are, and being embroiled in dramatic problems keeps us from having to hold still and find out. . . . We may cry and scream and weep and wail. But we are not able to use our emotions to guide us in making the necessary and important choices in our life."[1]

Survivors not only learn to disassociate themselves from painful emotions, but they also become overly pleasing to others. Such was the case for Valerie.

Valerie's father emotionally abused her all of her life; he abused her sexually from age eleven until she left home for college. Valerie learned early in life to please her father's every whim. Now a housewife and mother of teens, Valerie related, "One afternoon when I was about five my dad told me to get something from a neighbor's house. On my way out the door I stopped to watch something on television. It couldn't have delayed me more than a minute, but it angered my dad so much that he slapped my face—hard. He then pushed me off the back stoop down the steps. I landed on all fours in our backyard. My body hurt for days afterward. I always obeyed my father's demands promptly after that, trying to anticipate his every wish.

"I believed I was responsible for my dad's happiness," Valerie explained. "He and my mother didn't get along. They never sat down with me and discussed their problems or even acknowledged them, but they came close to separating on several occasions. As horrible as my experience was, my fear of my dad leaving and of us going hungry was worse."

Besides ignoring their emotions and becoming overly responsible to meet the wants and needs of others, survivors usually feel safest when giving and feel insecure or guilty when someone gives to them. They often find themselves attracted to needy people. If they have no problem or crisis to solve, life seems boring, empty, and worthless. Abuse victims often over-commit themselves and end up feeling harried and pressured. Some appear rigid and controlled in an effort to compensate for growing up in an out-of-control environment.

These coping mechanisms, a sampling of the codependent characteristics outlined in Melody Beattie's book, *Codependent No More*,[2] are ways survivors try to compensate for their faulty foundations that failed to provide them with a sense of love, competence, and worth. To experience God's re-parenting, survivors need to pinpoint the unhealthy coping mechanisms they have carried into adulthood. Only then can they break new ground, allowing God to lay his firm foundation in their lives.

CONFRONTING CORE ISSUES

The fear of confronting core issues prevents adults abused as children from breaking new ground in their lives. Core issues are painful emotions that survivors could never resolve as children. Such core issues include feeling inadequate, worthless, abandoned, unprotected, shamed, guilty, betrayed, and untrusting. We could diagram the difference between dysfunctional foundations and God's foundation this way:

Dysfunctional Blueprint Versus God's Blueprint

Dysfunctional Blueprint

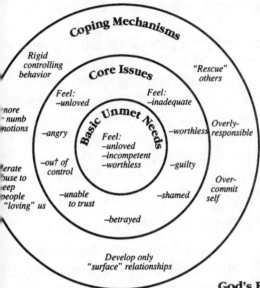

God's Blueprint

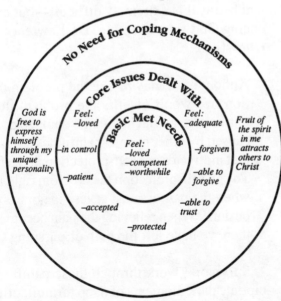

When Love Is Not Perfect

When the basic need for love, competence, and worth is not met, it is difficult to confront core issues. Instead, we develop self-protection devices that inevitably mask our true personality.

God's blueprint for family life provides a healthy foundation of love, competence, and worth. With such a solid foundation, we have no reason to fear confrontation with core issues and no need for unhealthy coping mechanisms. This foundation includes experiencing God's forgiveness and an ability to forgive others. As this foundation grows in us and our relationship with God deepens, the unique person he created in us shines forth and brings others into a knowledge of Christ.

WORKING THROUGH THE PAIN

Breaking new ground to implement God's foundational blueprint involves a confrontation with core issues. Getting in touch with painful feelings such as abandonment and betrayal is extremely difficult—but critical in experiencing God's re-parenting. Dr. Lawrence Crabb in *Inside Out* writes,

> Although we may *define* the problem of self-protection, we won't *identify* the problem in our own life until we're in touch with the damage done to our soul caused by other people's sinfulness, a painful damage that motivates our self-protection in the first place. . . . To call self-protection the problem right at the moment when the pain is most severe is not easy. But it must be done. When relieving the pain becomes our priority, then we have left the path of pursuing God.[3]

Survivors' work through these painful issues will precipitate dark moments of deep turmoil, often causing them to grapple with their view of God. When this happens, they need to surround themselves with the loving support of other Christians.

Dr. Charles Swindoll observes in *Dropping Your Guard*,

Periodically we'll have folks slip into our church who are in need of inner healing. They are spent. Hungry for a place to repair, they long for the freedom to be still and to gain renewed perspective. Such folks are to be respected and allowed some room to recover. They don't need somebody to corner them and 'put 'em to work.' In such cases, assimilation and involvement need to be put on hold. Their greater need (as in the case of Elijah) is to be allowed the freedom to relax.[4]

Some may find themselves "in need of repair." Others may be called upon to help a fellow Christian feel respected and find room to recover. As we learn to recognize coping mechanisms and confront core issues God will enable us to "break new ground," paving the way for him to lay his firm foundation in our lives and in the lives of others.

The next chapter will explore ways in which abuse distorts a person's image of God. When a survivor begins to build his life upon God's firm foundation, he is then ready for God to supply the beams for a solid framework. The lumber needed for this framing includes a right view of God and a deeper look at how he can re-parent us.

TIME TO CONSIDER

1. Do you often find it difficult to accept God's blueprint for your life?

2. How can you begin to embrace God's blueprint?

3. List the coping mechanisms mentioned in this chapter. Do you recognize any you employ? What prompts you to use them? Think back to your childhood. When did you first develop unhealthy coping mechanisms?

4. List the core issues mentioned in this chapter. Which ones do you find the most difficult to confront? Why?

GOD'S NURTURING WORDS TO YOU

"My child, as your Father, my eyes are on you, and my ears are attentive to your cry. I am close to the brokenhearted and save those who are crushed in spirit. As you let yourself feel your brokenheartedness, I will extend peace to you like a river. I will nurse you and carry you when necessary. As a mother comforts her child, so I will comfort you.

"Break up your unplowed ground and do not sow among thorns. Circumcise yourselves to the Lord; circumcise your hearts. Sow for yourselves righteousness, and reap the fruit of unfailing love. It is time to seek the Lord until he showers righteousness on you.

"I know the plans I have for you, even though things may seem confusing right now. My plans are to prosper you, not to harm you. I will give you hope and a future. But you must come to me. Seek me with all your heart and you will find me." (Paraphrased from Psalm 34:15-18; Isaiah 66:12, 13; Jeremiah 4:3, 4; Hosea 10:12; Jeremiah 29:11-14.)

Part III
A Solid Framework

5
...

Righting a Wrong View of God

When I first saw *Star Trek—The Movie*, I bristled at a line spoken by the captain. "We all make God in our own image," he declared. I wanted to stand up in the theater and shout: "No! Man was created in the image of God!"

Later I read Psalm 18:25, 26. "To the faithful you show yourself faithful, to the blameless you show yourself blameless, to the pure you show yourself pure, but to the crooked you show yourself shrewd." Those verses helped me understand that our particular approach to life can affect our view of God. We *can* perceive God in our own image.

God created us in his image, but the fall of man defaced that likeness. "So God created man in his own image, in the image of God he created him; male and female he created them" (Gen. 1:27). After Adam and Eve sinned, they later bore a son named Seth. "When Adam had lived 130 years, he had a son in his own likeness, in his own image" (Gen. 5:3). The stamp of God on Adam's children now included the element of free choice gone awry. Ever since, man has struggled between the poles of perceiving God in his own image and seeing God for who he really is.

DISTORTIONS OF GOD

Adults abused as children find it difficult to see God for who he really is because they grew up with dysfunctional family blueprints. Their abuse left cracks in their foundations of love, competence, and worth, making it difficult to develop solid frameworks upon which to build their lives. Common distortions survivors may hold of God include thoughts such as, "I'm too bad to deserve God's love." "He couldn't possibly accept me as I am." "He's not trustworthy." "He expects me to do things but doesn't give me the power to do them." "If I'm honest about my pain, God won't be there for me." Those abused as children can challenge these distortions with a right view of God.

Denise struggled with thoughts that she could never be good enough to deserve God's love and acceptance. Her parents physically abused her and her four brothers from the time they were babies until they left home. "Both of my parents came from alcoholic and physically abusive homes," Denise explained. "They'd pull down our pants and beat us with a belt or a switch. When I was fifteen my parents were on their way home from a bar and smashed into a tree. Dad was killed instantly, and Mom spent the next few months in a hospital recovering from a broken neck. After the accident she continued to drink. She eventually remarried and later divorced a neighbor with whom she had had an affair while my father was still alive.

"I believed I was a bad person—not that I just did bad things for which my parents beat me, but that *I* was bad. I thought God was mean and would end my life at any moment, throwing me into a burning fire. When I was eight a male baby-sitter began to sexually abuse me, and I felt I had no one to turn to. Every night my only prayer was that God would let me live one more day.

"My image of God changed when I began therapy with a Christian counselor," Denise continued. "She repeated things I needed to hear hundreds of times until my heart finally believed them. I could finally begin to believe in God's unconditional love. She validated that I was abused and that it was wrong. She helped me identify my dysfunctions and then prayed with me and for me about each issue. She gave me permission to feel what I had tried so hard not to feel for so long. As a result, I'm coming through on the other side of those feelings of anger, shame, worthlessness, and helplessness to healing and forgiveness."

Linda, emotionally and sexually abused from the age of three until twenty, found that her abuse made it difficult for her to trust God. "I'd been a Christian for several years, but not until I began to work through my abuse issues did I discover I didn't know how to let go and give God all of me," Linda explained.

"My image of God changed mostly because of my husband's response to me as I worked on recovering from the abuse." Linda paused and smiled. "My husband's unconditional love for me and tenacity to totally commit himself to me no matter what overwhelmed me. I'm learning to trust God each day, placing myself into the Lord's agenda instead of rushing ahead of him, trying to control everything. I used to feel like God asked me to do things but wouldn't give me the power to carry them out. Now I know that he won't ask me to do anything that he won't give me the power to do."

Besides feeling unacceptable to God, too bad to deserve his love, that he is not trustworthy, or that he expects us to do things without empowering us, many abuse victims also feel that if they embrace their pain, God won't be there for them. Such was the case for Rachel.

Rachel grew up with an alcoholic father and used anger to avoid her painful core issues of feeling abandoned, unprotected, and unable to trust. She shared: "One Sunday our pastor talked about a sermon by a famous preacher titled, 'Sinners in the Hands of an Angry God.' As I listened, I got more and more upset. Under my breath I muttered, 'Shut up, shut up!' I couldn't handle listening to our pastor talk about an angry God. Finally I left.

"To think God could be angry reminded me too much of my father and mother," she admitted. "As a child, I'd wake up at two or three in the morning to the sound of my parents screaming and fighting over my dad's drinking. As a result, I grew up picturing God as a big, non-caring person who would slap me down if I didn't toe the line. Now, as a Christian, I'm trying to cultivate my image of God as a loving Father. My pastor's sermon brought up a lot of painful emotions.

"I'm realizing," Rachel continued, "that if the intensity of my anger is inappropriate to the situation, as it was that Sunday morning, it's usually because I'm hitting up against a distortion in my view of God. Then I say to myself, 'Monster God Returns!' That phrase jokingly reminds me that I'm slipping into old coping patterns. Growing up, anger kept me from getting in touch with more painful issues such as feeling abandoned or unprotected. Unconsciously I might be telling myself, 'God doesn't really care about me.' Now I'm learning to process my anger instead of running from it, so I can get in touch with the core emotions hiding behind it. I'm slowly realizing that, as I work through those issues, God is still there for me, unlike my emotionally unavailable parents."

CHALLENGING DISTORTIONS

Abuse victims must recognize the ways in which their abuse has distorted their view of God, and challenge those distortions with the truth of God's Word. If their abuse left them feeling bad and unacceptable to God, they can challenge that lie with Ephesians 1:6. "He hath made us accepted in the beloved" (KJV).

Unlike abusive parents or caretakers, God is trustworthy and good. Psalm 119:68 says of God, "You are good, and what you do is good."

As for God not giving us the power to do what he wants, Philippians 2:13 says, "For it is God who works in you to will and to act according to his good purpose." And 1 Corinthians 10:13 promises that God will not let us be tempted beyond what we can bear, but rather provide a way out so that we can stand up under it.

We don't have to fear God's abandonment when we are honest with him about our pain because he desires truth in our innermost being. "Surely you desire truth in the inner parts; you teach me wisdom in the inmost place. . . . The sacrifices of God are a broken spirit; a broken and contrite heart, O God, you will not despise" (Ps. 51: 6, 17). As we courageously face our fears, God promises, "Never will I leave you; never will I forsake you" (Heb. 13:5).

"WITH ALL YOUR HEART, SOUL, AND MIND"

Survivors and those who support them through their recovery process must realize, however, that righting a wrong view of God involves more than the intellect.

Psychiatrist Joseph Wolpe writes, "Emotional habits are resistant to logical arguments or good advice, because something that is learned emotionally cannot be dealt with purely at an intellectual level."[1]

Jesus said the greatest commandment is to "Love the Lord your God with all your heart and with all your soul and with all your mind" (Matt. 22:37). Challenging distortions in our view of God must involve our whole being. Intellectually, we may need to repeatedly hear, as Denise did, the truth about God's love, justice, faithfulness, and compassion. Emotionally, we need to know that God longs to be gracious to us, to show us he is the God of compassion (Isa. 30:18). And we must choose with our wills to challenge our misconceptions with the truth God has revealed to us through his Word.

NAOMI AND *EL SHADDAI*

Naomi, whose story is found in the Old Testament book of Ruth, knew what it meant to get in touch with painful issues. Although not abused, Naomi suffered the loss of a husband and two sons. Deprived of any grandchildren, she had no one to provide for her in her old age. When she arrived back in Bethlehem from Moab without her husband and sons, the women of the town exclaimed, " 'Can this be Naomi?'

" 'Don't call me Naomi,' she told them. 'Call me Mara, because the Almighty has made my life very bitter. I went away full, but the Lord has brought me back empty' " (Ruth 1:19, 20).

Naomi's name meant pleasant. But she asked her former neighbors to call her Mara, meaning bitter, because she had felt the bitter sting of loneliness, of having no one to protect her or care for her.

Irony is expressed in her choice of words for God. "The

Almighty (*El Shaddai*) has made my life very bitter." The Hebrew word *Shaddai* is close to the Hebrew word used for "breast."[2] In the past, Naomi had known God as one who nourished and satisfied, but now she knew him as one who had made her life bitter.

Although Naomi's faith in God as *El Shaddai* was shaken, she continued to put her trust in him and his Word because he had been faithful in the past. When her husband and sons died, instead of remaining desolate in Moab, Naomi moved back to Bethlehem to be with her own people.

In Bethlehem, she put her deceased husband's and sons' lands up for sale. Naomi knew that God's law required the kinsman who purchased a deceased man's land to acquire his widow as well. With this in mind, Naomi prompted her daughter-in-law, Ruth, who returned with her to Bethlehem from Moab, to seek out one of their kinsmen, Boaz.

In the book of Ruth, Naomi's friends never called her Mara. Naomi got in touch with her lonely, abandoned feelings, but she never acted on them. Instead, she took steps to see God's promises fulfilled in her life. Her waiting on God was rewarded. In Ruth 4 we read that Boaz took Ruth as his wife, and she gave birth to a son.

"The women said to Naomi, 'Praise be to the Lord, who this day has not left you without a kinsman-redeemer. May he become famous throughout Israel! He will renew your life and sustain you in your old age. . . .'

"Then Naomi took the child, laid him in her lap and cared for him" (Ruth 4:14-16). The King James version translates verse 16, "And Naomi took the child, and laid it in her bosom, and became nurse unto it."

Naomi could nurture others because she experienced God as *El Shaddai*, the breasted One, her sustainer. She honestly shared her pain with those close to her but acted on God's Word rather than on her emotions.

As abuse victims get in touch with their painful emotions and challenge their distortions of God with the truth of the Bible, they can embrace a right view of God with all of their heart, soul, and mind. A healthy view of God will help them erect solid frameworks and roofs of protection for their lives, enabling them to experience God's re-parenting.

TIME TO CONSIDER

1. What makes it difficult for adults abused as children to have an accurate view of God?

2. Name some common distortions abuse victims may have of God?

3. Can you identify with any of the distortions? Do you have other false concepts of God not mentioned in this chapter?

4. Did you find the scripture passages mentioned in this chapter helpful? Which ones? Why?

5. What steps did Naomi take to move her from Mara, one who was bitter, to Naomi, "pleasant"—one who experienced God's *El Shaddai* nurturing?

6. Where are you in this process? What actions can you take to move to the next step?

GOD'S NURTURING WORDS TO YOU

"As you get in touch with painful events from the past, you may feel bitter and cry out to me, 'Why did my way seem hidden to you?' My child, I am the everlasting God, the Creator of the ends of the earth, the One who measured the waters in the hollow of my hand. I bring out the starry host one by one and call them each by name. Because of my great power and mighty strength, not one of them is missing. No one can fathom the depths of my knowledge and understanding.

"I long to be gracious to you; I rise to show you compassion. I am a God of justice, the God of the womb, and your *El Shaddai*. Blessed are all those who wait for me." (Paraphrased from Isaiah 40:27-30, 12, 26; 30:18.)

6
...

The Nurturing Side of God

When a writing friend told me that at age eighteen he had changed his legal name, I was curious. I discovered his name change had nothing to do with writing. Rather, it expressed his desire for re-parenting.

Joe, born in 1928, grew up with a verbally abusive mother and an emotionally distant father. "As a child," Joe related, "my favorite radio program was 'One Man's Family.' I wished someone like the character in the show, Paul Barbour, would adopt me. In one episode, Mr. Barbour did adopt someone—a girl. I was devastated because he didn't adopt me.

"During our childhood," Joe continued, "if my younger brother, sister, and I didn't behave, my parents threatened that the bogeyman would get us. I believed my parents and grew up fearing the dark since that was when the bogey-man supposedly came out. One evening when I was five or six, my brother, sister and I did something wrong. Mom and Dad ushered us outside, turned off the lights, and locked the doors. We screamed and pounded on the doors, begging them to let us in. I'm sure my parents eventually unlocked the doors, but I don't remember that part.

"We attended a nearby church where my dad was baptized, but it didn't have much effect on his life. Mom accused Dad of laziness and sleeping around with women. One night my father had enough. He hit Mom over the head with a stool, breaking it to pieces.

"I could never live up to my parents' expectations," Joe explained. "Mom's words seared me: 'You're so lazy—just like your father!' Dad wanted me to be a macho football star and to love country and western music, but I enjoyed books and favored classical music. When I turned eighteen, I changed my name to get away from my heritage. Until three years ago, I couldn't even tell people my given name.

"My family affected the way I viewed God," Joe said. "My early church experience and my relationship with my father made me feel like God was distant and didn't care about me—especially after my parents divorced. Even now I sometimes struggle when I pray, plagued by the thought, *God has more important things to do than to listen to me.*

"In college I was exhausted and depressed. I sought counseling. But real change didn't occur until years later when I counseled with a Christian therapist. During one of our sessions, I related the extreme hurt I felt when the radio character, Paul Barbour, adopted someone else instead of me. Then, as if an explosion went off inside of me, I blurted out, 'But I *have* been adopted!' For years I had known intellectually that God had adopted me into his family when I put my faith in Christ. But suddenly my heart knew it too."

THE GOD WHO ADOPTS US

We take the first step in experiencing God's re-parenting when we understand that God has adopted us. Joe knew this as a child but did not grasp its full meaning until he shared the pain of his abusive upbringing with his Christian counselor. Suddenly, God's adoption took on new meaning for him. Ephesians 1:5, 6 explains, "He predestined us to be adopted as his sons through Jesus Christ, in accordance with his pleasure and will—to the praise of his glorious grace, which he has freely given us in the One he loves."

The Greek word used in Ephesians 1:6 for grace is *charis*. Joe, a graduate student of Applied Theology and author of *Rediscovering Passover*, explained that this first century Greek word, *charis*, expressed the favor shown someone when they were adopted into a Greek or Roman family. If a free Greek or Roman saw someone who had great potential as an athlete, scholar, artist, or, in the case of the fictional character Ben Hur, a chariot racer, the Greek or Roman would officially adopt that person into his family and sponsor his education. So, too, God has placed great potential within each one of us. When we receive Christ, God adopts us into his family and desires to nurture us, protect us, and develop our potential for his glory.

THE GOD WHO IS WHOLLY WITH US

As God's adopted children, *all* of God is with us *all* of the time. We don't just have a "piece" of him. John 20:15-17 relates the story of Jesus' appearance to Mary Magdalene after he rose from the dead. " 'Woman,' he said, 'why are you crying? Who is it you are looking for?'

"Thinking he was the gardener, she said, 'Sir, if you have carried him away, tell me where you have put him, and I will get him.'

"Jesus said to her, 'Mary.'

"She turned toward him and cried out in Aramaic, 'Rabboni!' (which means Teacher).

"Jesus said, 'Do not hold on to me, for I have not yet returned to the Father.' "

Later, after the disciples had seen Jesus ascend into heaven, they waited in an upper room as he had instructed them. "Suddenly a sound like the blowing of a violent wind came from heaven and filled the whole house where they were sitting. They saw what seemed to be tongues of fire that separated and came to rest on each of them. All of them were filled with the Holy Spirit and began to speak in other tongues as the Spirit enabled them" (Acts 2:2-4).

Jesus could only be in one place at one time while he walked this earth. That's why he asked Mary not to hold on to him. He had to ascend to his Father so he could send the Holy Spirit to dwell within each believer.

The tongues of fire referred to in Acts would have reminded a Jewish believer of God's presence that filled the tent of meeting and later filled Solomon's temple (Ex. 40:34-38, Lev. 9:23, and 2 Chron. 7:1).

In the same way, now that Jesus has offered the perfect sacrifice for sins through his death on the cross, God sends the Holy Spirit to come and wholly dwell within each believer as we put our faith in him (1 Cor. 3:16).

"Knowing that God is wholly with me," Joe shared, "made me realize God cares about me as an individual." Colossians 2:9 tells us that in Christ "all the fulness of Deity lives in bodily form. . . ." So, too, the fulness of God dwells within us when we are adopted into God's family and have his Holy Spirit dwelling within us.

PRESENCE, PERMISSION, AND PASSAGE

Adults abused as children can know God's nurture as they grasp the truth of their adoption and understand that his presence dwells wholly within them through his Holy Spirit. They will also experience the nurturing side of God's character as they put themselves in his presence, give him permission to bring them face to face with their painful emotions, and allow his passage through their lives so he can heal their scarred emotions.

Presence

One Sunday afternoon I sat down to read the newspaper, hoping to escape a gnawing sense of anger I felt welling up inside of me. I couldn't put my finger on what had precipitated my frustration, but I couldn't seem to shake it. As I glanced through the paper, a picture of a toddler sitting in the rubble of his bombed house caught my attention. The little Lebanese boy clutched a few toys under his arm as the camera snapped his bewildered expression. The picture made something in me snap. I cried, identifying with the unsettling emotions the boy must have experienced.

We had recently bought a home in a new city. We were hurting financially because our previous landlord would not let us out of our year's lease. Shortly after, my husband, Mark, fell at work and fractured his elbow. We weren't sure if he could continue working while his elbow healed, or if the injury would force him to take a sick leave, resulting in a cut in pay. To top it off, my fibrositis constantly made my muscles feel as if they were on fire, making it difficult to sleep at night.

I felt hurt and betrayed by our previous landlord. Our unstable financial condition and my husband's injury made me feel insecure and fearful. My inability to control my pain angered me. Emotions were magnified because I was working through my own abuse issues at the time. I had gotten in touch with core issues of feeling betrayed, unprotected, abandoned, and fearful, and those raw emotions weren't ready to take on my present situation. Looking at the Lebanese boy's face as he sat in the rubble of his house clutching his little toys under his arm brought everything to the surface.

We attended church that night, but I sat in the pew with my arms folded across my chest, refusing to sing. The congregation sang the chorus: "Nothing can separate us from his love . . . not our past. . . ." I didn't hear any more of the song after those words penetrated. Tears streamed down my face. My husband looked at me in dismay, but I couldn't talk right then. I realized I had let my past separate me from God's love. I silently confessed that to God, unfolded my arms, and sang through my tears. I chose to put myself in God's presence and asked him to wash away my pain and bind up my wounds.

Permission

We also experience God's nurture as we give him permission to bring painful issues to the surface. Hosea 6:1 says, "Come, let us return to the Lord. He has torn us to pieces but he will heal us; he has injured us but he will bind our wounds."

To help pay for his college education, my husband worked in a cafeteria. One day a fellow worker accidentally spilled scalding hot water on Mark's foot. He tended his burn by bandaging it during the day and letting it air at night. The burn scabbed over but never healed properly. When Mark finally saw a doctor, he learned that the scab covered a festering infection. The doctor lanced Mark's foot, drained the infection, cleansed the wound, and bandaged it once again. The doctor instructed him to leave the bandage on, night and day, for at least a week. After Mark removed the bandage a week later, he discovered that, although his foot was still sensitive, the burn had completely healed.

In the same way, abuse victims carry around festering emotional wounds hidden underneath layers of defense mechanisms. When they give God permission to open up and cleanse their wounds, he can then properly bandage them and bring about his healing.

Passage

A third aspect of God's nurturing includes allowing his passage in our lives. A few months after I began to work on my abuse issues, I woke up in the middle of the night and couldn't go back to sleep. An event that happened when I was about six or seven came to mind.

I recalled my father setting up a tent in our backyard. Since it was a hot summer evening and I had never slept in a tent before, I was enthused about the project. As soon as Dad had the tent up, I darted into the house to tell my mother. I relayed my message and dashed toward the screen door, hand extended, intending to push it open. But I'd neglected to unlatch it. My hand crashed through the upper glass portion of the door.

I screamed and ran to my mom, holding out my bloody hand. She picked the pieces of glass out of my flesh, washed off my hand under cold water, and bandaged it up. She then asked a twelve-year-old neighbor to take me for a walk around the block because she couldn't handle my crying.

As I recalled the incident, my throat and chest tightened. "I don't want to go for a walk!" I cried, as if I were that little girl once again, talking to my mother. "I just want you to hold me on your lap! I want you to stroke my hair, to rock me and tell me that you know my hand must hurt very much."

Getting in touch with the hurt little girl inside and hearing her, for the first time, voice her emotional pain, frightened me. I had never done that before. But as I let myself feel the hurt, I sensed God's presence. I looked at the hand I had injured and fingered a scar I still carry from that accident. Suddenly a scripture came to mind and I prayed it back to God. "Yet I am always with you; you hold me by my right hand. You guide me with your counsel" (Ps. 73:23, 24).

I pictured God taking hold of my scarred right hand. Then it hit me. His hand had a scar too! I felt what I call God's passage as I pictured Jesus' nail-scarred hand holding my scarred hand. Like sipping a cup of hot chocolate on a chilly winter morning, God passed through my life with his cleansing and caring presence. He then bandaged up my emotional wounds with the balm of his Spirit.

Abuse survivors need to experience the nurturing side of God's character. This will happen as they become adopted into his family and allow him to develop the potential he has placed within them. Knowing God is wholly with them can counter thoughts such as, *How could God really care about me?* with the knowledge that they are a temple of the Holy Spirit. And as survivors put themselves in God's presence with arms unfolded, giving him permission to cleanse and bind up their hurts, they will then experience his healing passage moving through their lives like a gentle wind.

With such a framework and roof of protection in place, survivors of abuse can begin to put up walls and windows. These structures show them how to set proper boundaries in their relationships with others, and yet maintain a vulnerability that contributes not only to their own growth, but also the growth of others. The next section will focus on these issues.

TIME TO CONSIDER

1. Read John 1:12, 13 and 1 John 5:11-13. How can we know if we have eternal life and are truly children of God?

2. What does the Greek word *charis* mean?

3. Read Ephesians 1:5, 6. What did adoption mean in New Testament times? How does that relate to God's adoption of us?

4. Read Ephesians 1:13, 14. What do we receive when we put our trust in Christ for our salvation?

5. Read John 16:15, 16. What does the Holy Spirit do for us?

6. What are some ways we can put ourselves in God's presence?

7. Can you think of an incident when it was difficult for you to give God permission to work his will in your life? What can help you give him permission to move in your life as he wishes? (See John 15:1-4 and Hebrews 10:23, 24 for some ideas.)

8. Think of an incident when you experienced God's passage in your life. What part does scripture play in experiencing God's passage? (See Psalm 119:72-77, 92, 93, 105; Hebrews 4:12.)

GOD'S NURTURING WORDS TO YOU

"You are fearfully and wonderfully made. When I knit you together in your mother's womb, your form was not hidden from me. My eyes saw your unformed body. At that time all the days of your life were ordained by me, written in my book before one of them ever came to be. Thoughts of you are precious to me. If you were to count the number of times I think about you, the sum would outnumber the grains of sand.

"Yes, I created you, but I also adopted you as my child. Embrace the forgiveness I extend to your through my Son, Jesus, and you will know my nurturing love. As my child, I will put the Spirit of my Son within your heart, enabling you to call out to me, 'Abba, Father—Papa.'

"At times you may feel like I am tearing you to pieces. But you must give me permission to open up and cleanse your wounds. If you press on to know me, then, as surely as the sun arises, I will come to you. I will come like the winter rains, like the spring rains that water the earth. You will know my passage. You will know my healing." (Paraphrased from Psalm 139:13-18; Ephesians 1:5, 6; John 1:12; Galatians 4:6; Hosea 6:1-3.)

Part IV

Walls and Windows

7
...

Setting Boundaries

Jill's stepfather sexually abused her from the time she was eleven until she began her second year of college. At age seventeen, she gave birth to his child and lied to her mother about the identity of the baby's father. She feared that telling her mother about her stepfather's incestuous relationship with her would result in the loss of the family's income. When he still pursued her sexually after the birth of his child, Jill couldn't take any more and became suicidal. Earlier that year, however, Jill had attended a church where, for the first time, she'd heard about the love and forgiveness of God.

"I looked at myself in the mirror, sleeping pills in hand," Jill shared, "and decided not to take them. Instead, I got into bed where I told God that if he really was everything that I had heard about him at church, then I'd live the rest of my life for him. The next morning he gave me the courage to tell my mom the truth about my stepdad."

At age eleven, Jill had no idea how to set boundaries that would prevent her stepfather's advances. Now that she has two teen-aged daughters of her own, however, Jill has learned to set firm boundaries. "Even now when I visit my mom and stepfather," she said, "I catch my stepdad giving me lustful looks. My daughters don't know about the abuse, but I never leave them alone with him, and we only visit on family occasions when my husband is with us."

The walls of a home provide security, warmth, and protection. Adults abused as children had their boundaries violated early in life. As a result, many abuse victims find it difficult to establish healthy boundaries. Some wall themselves off from others, relating to people only on a surface level. Others fail to set any boundaries at all, frantically running around trying to meet everyone's needs. How can survivors set healthy boundaries for themselves?

GIVING FOR THE WRONG REASONS

The abuse that Kate experienced as a child made it difficult for her to set boundaries. She could not distinguish where her responsibilities ended and someone else's began.

During her childhood, Kate's father often beat her mother, and Kate would wash and bandage the wounds. Now, as an adult, Kate shared, "It's difficult to set boundaries. My parents were so caught up in their own pain that my needs were not met. Their needs became my needs. Even when my parents were in their sixties, Mom would call and say, 'We had another fight. I'm afraid of what he'll do.' I'd rush to my mother's house, leaving my own family behind. I felt I had to do it—that I was responsible for my parents' pain as well as for their happiness. I also did this with any needy person I met."

Kate has begun to recognize where her responsibilities end and another's begin as she determines her God-given priorities. "I know I'm giving for the wrong reasons," Kate said, "when I give in order to avoid feeling the pain of my own unmet needs. As a child, I always gave to my parents, hoping I'd get their love. Now I realize that they did the best they could. They just weren't capable of giving me what I needed. I can stop 'rescuing' needy people, hoping to get the love I never got, because now I'm looking to God to provide my needs."

Besides giving in hopes of getting their own needs met or to avoid getting in touch with their own pain, abuse victims can also give to others to feel in "control" and gain a measure of self-worth. Therapist Robin Norwood explains, "Living in any of the more chaotic types of dysfunctional families such as an alcoholic, violent, or incestuous one, a child will inevitably feel panic at the family's loss of control. . . . By being strong and helpful to others we protect ourselves from the panic that comes from being at another's mercy. We need to be with people whom we can help, in order to feel safe and in control."[1]

So weak boundaries occur when abuse victims give to others for the wrong reasons. They develop a "rescuer" mentality in hopes of getting their own needs met or to avoid feeling the pain of unmet needs. Their giving may also mask an unhealthy desire to feel in control and worthwhile.

GIVING FOR THE RIGHT REASONS

Biblical passages such as Isaiah 58:10, 11 seem to sanction the "rescuer" mentality. "If you spend yourselves in behalf of the hungry and satisfy the needs of the oppressed, then your light will rise in the darkness, and your night will become like the noonday. The Lord will guide you always; he will satisfy your needs in a sun-scorched land and will strengthen your frame. You will be like a well-watered garden, like a spring whose waters never fail."

Luke 6:38 promises, "Give, and it will be given to you. A good measure, pressed down, shaken together and running over, will be poured into your lap." These passages admonish us to give and promise God's rewards for our acts of charity.

A problem arises, however, when we give out of our need rather than out of *God's abundance*. Second Corinthians 9:7 tells us, "Each man should give what he has decided in his heart to give, not reluctantly or under compulsion, for God loves a cheerful giver." Giving for the wrong reasons distracts us from letting God meet our needs. Only when we learn to give cheerfully, and not reluctantly or under compulsion, can we truly experience God's rewards. If you're unsure of your motives for giving, you might ask yourself, "Why should I be the one to do this task?"

SERVICE THAT DISTRACTS OR ATTRACTS

Giving for the right reasons helps us establish healthy boundaries. Instead of distracting us from our needs, our giving will attract people to God and make our relationship with him and others stronger. Two sisters in the Bible, Martha and Mary, illustrate the balance between meeting the needs of others and meeting our own needs.

Martha, a friend of Jesus who met his needs for food and shelter on several occasions, knew what it felt like to give for the wrong reasons. Luke 10:38-42 relates one of these episodes.

"As Jesus and his disciples were on their way, he came to a village where a woman named Martha opened her home to him. She had a sister called Mary, who sat at the Lord's feet listening to what he said. But Martha was distracted by all the preparations that had to be made. She came to him and asked, 'Lord, don't you care that my sister has left me to do the work by myself? Tell her to help me!'

" 'Martha, Martha,' the Lord answered, 'you are worried and upset about many things, but only one thing is needed. Mary has chosen what is better, and it will not be taken away from her.' "

A peek into Martha's kitchen window shows us that she was distracted by all the preparations she had to make. The Greek word for distracted, *perispao*, means to drag all around, to be drawn away or over-occupied.

I remember trying to carry on a conversation with a guest as I prepared dinner for her family and mine. While we talked, I cut and cooked the meat, reminded myself not to forget the rolls, and read the directions for making a sauce. Suddenly I caught myself asking my guest the same question twice. Realizing my distraction, I took a deep breath and re-focused on the purpose of our meal—getting to know my new friend and her family better.

Martha's pre-occupation with serving made her lose sight of Jesus' character and the value of spending time with him. "Lord," she asked Jesus, "don't you care that my sister has left me to do the work by myself?" (Luke 10:40).

Martha's attempt to control too many things at one time caused her to snap at Jesus. Not only had Mary abandoned her, but Martha felt as if even Jesus had abandoned her.

Jesus helped Martha pinpoint her problem. "Martha, Martha," the Lord answered, "you are worried and upset about many things" (Luke 10:41). Martha's serving goals pushed her in too many different directions. As a result, she got upset. "Only one thing is needed," Jesus reminded her (Luke 10:42). This doesn't mean that Jesus and his disciples didn't need to eat. Meeting their needs, however, in a clamorous way that distracted from the greater need to develop a closer relationship with Jesus, wasn't the best choice at that moment. Jesus explained to Martha, "Mary has chosen what is better, and it will not be taken away from her" (Luke 10:42).

The Greek word *eklegomai* used to describe Mary's choosing combined *ek*, meaning out, and *lego*, meaning to link and knit together one's inward thoughts and feelings.[2] Mary's thoughts and feelings were integrated. Because of that, she could decide what was the most important task at that moment.

Martha's confused thoughts and feelings dragged her around in circles, crippling her ability to organize her thoughts and choose the most beneficial activity at that moment.

If our serving "drags us around," distracts us from our own needs and walk with God, and feeds an unhealthy desire to control others, then we're serving for the wrong reasons, and we will have weak boundaries. If, however, while giving we can still think clearly and make wise choices for ourselves and those close to us, then our service will attract others to God and make our relationship with him and others stronger.

Healthy boundaries enable us to fulfill our God-given responsibilities. When our walls are properly placed, we can experience the warmth, security, and love only God can provide. The next chapter explores ways in which abuse prevents us from putting windows in our house and outlines steps we can take allowing God's love to penetrate the dark corners of our confused and scarred emotions.

TIME TO CONSIDER

1. What are some wrong reasons for giving to others? Can you share examples of incidents where you've either done this or seen this happen? What was the outcome?

2. What happened when Martha gave for the wrong reasons? How can you apply this in your own life?

3. How might passages such as Isaiah 58:10, 11 and Luke 6:38 be misinterpreted?

4. According to 2 Corinthians 9:7, how can we know when we're giving for the right reasons?

5. Think of some times when you or others you know seemed to give for the right reasons. What was the outcome? How did it affect you and those around you?

6. Write a prayer asking God to help you establish healthy boundaries. State specific areas where you find it most difficult to set boundaries. Find someone with whom you can share your prayer and who will encourage you to take steps in this direction.

GOD'S NURTURING WORDS TO YOU

"Like Martha, you sometimes run around in too many directions, desperately trying to elude your painful emotions of feeling abandoned and unprotected as a child. Your efforts to control the actions of others and the outcome of events leaves you feeling frustrated and depressed.

"My child, I urge you to come to me. To those who are

weary and burdened, I promise to give rest. Take my yoke upon you and learn from me, for I am gentle and humble in heart. In contrast to the weight you put upon your shoulders, my yoke is easy and my burden is light.

"Slow down long enough to sort out your tumultuous, confused thoughts and emotions. Only then will you be able to choose what is best. Only then will you truly be able to deny yourself, take up your cross, and follow me. If you learn to give for the right reasons, then your light will rise in the darkness. I will guide you and satisfy your needs in a sun-scorched land and strengthen your frame. You will be like a well-watered garden, like a spring whose waters never fail." (Paraphrased from Matthew 11:28-30; Luke 10:42; 9:23; Isaiah 58:10, 11.)

8

...

Opening Windows

When a tornado sweeps through a town, people often crack open their windows. This helps balance the air pressure inside with the air pressure outside. Otherwise, a tornado may rip off a house's roof or cause the entire structure to explode. So, too, abuse survivors can keep their inner lives from exploding when they learn how to open the windows to let in God's nurturing and to experience healthy interaction with others.

The sexual, physical, and emotional abuse Ginnie experienced as a child caused her to set boundaries close to herself. She avoided showering in her junior high school gym class because she didn't want anyone to see her bruises. "I wasn't embarrassed for me," Ginnie explained. "I thought I deserved the beatings. But I felt I'd have to explain that my parents hit me because I deserved it.

"The abuse, however," Ginnie said, "made me set boundaries close to myself. When I was young I remember someone saying to my parents, 'She is such a pretty child. Think of how she'll look when she grows up.' That frightened me. I didn't like people paying attention to me. I reasoned that the more invisible I felt, the less abuse I'd experience.

"Because I had become suspicious of kindness as a child," Ginnie continued, "now, as an adult, I find it difficult to accept compliments and kindness from others. I feel more comfortable appearing strong and confident, as if I don't need other people. I'm discovering, however, that if I put up walls to keep out the hurt, I keep out the good feelings, too."

Windows let in light. When we follow God's blueprint, our windows allow God's light to penetrate our lives. Jesus said, "I am the light of the world. Whoever follows me will never walk in darkness, but will have the light of life" (John 8:12).

Windows also let in fresh air. As we open our windows to God, the Holy Spirit, depicted in Acts 2:2 as wind, can blow his fresh, transforming power into our lives.

Windows allow us to view what's happening outside and give other people a glimpse inside our home. Adults abused as children need to draw back the curtains of their lives, allowing interaction with others. This will contribute not only to their own growth, but also to the growth of others. Ephesians 4:11-16 says that it's only as each person in the body of Christ uses his spiritual gift for the service of others that we will become "mature, attaining to the whole measure of the fullness of Christ."

Survivors who find it difficult to open up their windows to God and others can overcome their reluctance as they learn to keep current with their emotions; understand intellectually *and* emotionally that God will never abandon them; recognize the unhealthy ways they abandon themselves; and challenge their fears in specific ways.

Keep current with your emotions

Ginnie learned to keep current with her emotions by tuning in to things that made her feel uncomfortable. "One night at Bible study," Ginnie said, "one of the guys said I had a good singing voice. The group asked me to sing a solo, which I did, but I felt very uncomfortable. Singing in front of them isn't what made me feel ill at ease. Their kindness in asking me to sing made me uncomfortable because I never received much kindness as a child."

You can stay in touch with your emotions by tuning in to your body's clues. Does a certain situation or person cause your muscles to tighten up? What makes you feel happy or relaxed? Ask God to give you understanding about what makes you feel uncomfortable, tense, relaxed, or happy. Seek him to help you work through difficult emotions and to give you the freedom of his Spirit to help you enjoy moments of relaxation or celebration.

Feedback from others also helps us tune into our feelings. After church one Sunday I stopped to talk with Lisa, a friend who knew of my emotional pain as I worked through abuse issues. My two-year-old almost leaped out of my arms when he saw Lisa. She baby-sat for Daniel often, and he liked her very much. A few days later Lisa asked me how I had felt when Daniel sprang from my arms to embrace her.

"I think it's great!" I told her. "I'm glad he feels so comfortable with you."

"That's not what the look on your face said," Lisa responded. "When Daniel gave me that big hug, your expression changed immediately, as if you felt hurt that he wanted to come to me."

As I re-played the event in my mind, I felt a twinge of pain in my stomach. Daniel's response to Lisa *had* made me feel rejected. My facial expression revealed the emotion, although I was unaware of it at the time.

We keep current with our emotions as we open up our windows to God's light and the breath of his Spirit. Honest interaction with others also provides us with important feedback, cluing us in to emotions we may have repressed.

Understand that God will never abandon you

Have you ever felt so certain about a fact that you could say, "I *know* that I know"? Abuse victims need to know, not just intellectually, but emotionally, that God will never abandon them.

As a new Christian I memorized Colossians 2:10: "In Him you have been made complete" (NASB). At that time I had no conscious memory of childhood abuse, but I knew I felt incomplete and abandoned. When my college sweetheart told me he had met someone else and wanted to break off our relationship, I anchored my sinking soul in the truth that God had made me complete in Christ.

Later, when flashbacks of my dance teacher's sexual abuse surfaced, I felt as if someone had burrowed a deep hole into my being. The fear I had repressed for more than thirty years overwhelmed me. When I let myself feel the painful feelings of that event, however, I gained a new understanding of God's presence and protection. I found myself singing "O God Our Help in Ages Past." The second verse suddenly took on new meaning for me.

"Under the shadow of thy throne
    still may we dwell secure;
sufficient is Thine arm alone,

and our defense is sure."

For the first time I identified with the confidence Paul expressed in 2 Corinthians 4:8, 9, "We are . . . persecuted, but not abandoned." I had known before that God would never abandon me, but now I *knew* that I knew.

We must open the windows to our emotions, even if it means getting in touch with painful feelings we've avoided all of our lives. When we do, we will also let in God's nurture and understand emotionally as well as intellectually that he will never abandon us.

Recognize how you abandon yourself

Rachel's story of growing up in an alcoholic home and the resulting emotional abuse is found in chapter 5. She explained how the phrase "Monster God Returns" helps her recognize and deal with circumstances that make her feel as if God has abandoned her. She finds it more difficult, however, to recognize and confront the ways she abandons herself.

"Right now one of my biggest problems is over-eating," Rachel confided. "A while ago I took a course called 'Thin Within' but never completed it. In one of our sessions we shared a meal together. We had to tell each other how the food made us feel and when we felt full. Getting in tune with messages from my body threatened me. I feared that my body would say I was full before I had eaten enough to satisfy me emotionally. I realize now that I disassociate myself from my physical body. I view my body as an 'it' rather than as a part of me."

Any physically harmful activity such as over-eating, anorexia, bulimia, taking drugs, or consuming alcohol may evidence a person's self-abandonment. Unfortunately, self-abandonment through food, drugs, or alcohol is not easily overcome because of their addictive natures.

When Love Is Not Perfect

Therapist Robin Norwood discovered that many of her clients who did not develop alcoholism, but had alcoholic parents, developed food addictions. She also points out that refined sugar is not a food but a drug. Along with drugs and alcohol, it can dramatically alter brain chemistry and is a highly addicting substance for many people.[1] Self-abandonment must be dealt with on all levels: intellectual, physical, emotional, and spiritual.

Challenge your fears in specific ways

Ginnie discovered that, at age thirty-six, she didn't really know how to make friends.

"I mentioned to one of the girls in our Singles' Group that I never seemed to hear about the social events. Her response surprised me. She said that she thought I had it all together and didn't need friends. I'm realizing now I really *do* need people," Ginnie admitted. "The more I get to know others, the better I get to know God as I see him through them. It's not a lesser dependence of God, but a widening of that dependence through people."

Now, instead of always trying to appear strong, Ginnie is slowly beginning to share some of her weaknesses and hurts with others she feels she can trust. It has taken her a while to feel comfortable extending herself in words. She found it easier through deeds, like baking an extra batch of cookies for someone or writing a note. "For my own protection, I didn't want to open all my windows at once," Ginnie explained. "Learning to trust others and be a friend isn't a one-time event. It's a process. I'm taking it a step at a time."

Once we recognize the fears that keep us from opening up to God and others, we can take small, specific steps in that direction. "Those who grew up in dysfunctional families are good at being what other people want them to be," says Dr. Philip Kavanaugh, a psychiatrist in Los Gatos, California, who works with survivors. "I encourage my patients to get into Twelve-Step groups because they need to learn how to be part of a group that accepts them just as they are. If you can become a part of a group not because they like your personality, or because you're giving them what they want—trying to win their affection as you did in your dysfunctional family—then you can eventually widen your world as you work through being who you are with others outside of that group."

For some, a first step in working through who they are may be telling God how they honestly feel. Others may take steps in opening their windows by writing someone an encouraging note or by phoning a friend when they need help. Others may join a Bible study or a Twelve-Step group.[2]

God's love can penetrate the dark corners of our confused and scarred emotions when we learn how to keep current with our emotions, understand that God won't abandon us, recognize the unhealthy ways we abandon ourselves, and challenge our fears in specific ways. All of this may seem overwhelming. Remember, recovery is a process. Focus on one area at a time, trusting God to accomplish his good work in you. Philippians 1:6 reminds us that *God* is the one who does the completing. ". . . being confident of this, that he who began a good work in you will carry it on to completion until the day of Christ Jesus."

As we learn to set healthy boundaries by putting walls and windows into place, we can then look for new furniture. The next section will examine what it means to become like a little child, re-parented by God, in order to experience the kingdom of heaven. We will also look at the Holy Spirit's role in transforming our body, soul, and spirit as we move toward growing in wholeness.

TIME TO CONSIDER

1. How can abuse influence a person to set boundaries close to himself, closing off areas of his life from others? Where are your boundaries?

2. What are the benefits of opening up our lives to God and to others?

3. What does it mean to "keep current with your emotions"? What are some practical ways we can do this?

4. How can the following biblical references help you understand that God will never abandon you? John 10:27-30; 2 Timothy 2:13; Hebrews 13:5.

5. Think of a time when you felt secure. What made you feel that way? When did you feel the most insecure or unprotected? What made you feel that way? How can the knowledge that God will never abandon you deepen your sense of security or help when you feel insecure or unprotected?

6. Can you think of other ways people might evidence unhealthy self-abandonment besides through eating disorders, drugs, or alcohol? Can you identify with any of these? How can opening up our lives to God and others help us overcome these self-destructive habits?

GOD'S NURTURING WORDS TO YOU

"My child, take time to let my words penetrate the dark corners or your confused and scarred emotions. As a deer pants for streams of water, so I desire that your soul would pant for me, the living God. Let the tears flow, even if they seem to be your food day and night. Pour out your soul to me.

"By day I will direct my love to you. At night my song will be with you. My son did not say, 'Blessed are those who ignore their hurt,' but rather, 'Blessed are those who *mourn*, for they will be comforted.'

"No one can snatch you out of my hand. Keep your heart open to me. Even if you are faithless at times, I will remain faithful to you. Be open also to the people I may put in your path to encourage you and to help bind up your hurts. Through them, through my Word, and through my Spirit, I will never leave you or forsake you. Rest secure in the arms of my love." (Paraphrased from Psalm 42:1-4; Psalm 42:8; Matthew 5:4; John 10:29; 2 Timothy 2:13; Hebrews 13:5.)

Part V

New Furniture

9
...

Like a Little Child

Adults abused as children can build their lives upon a firm foundation as God meets their needs for love, worth, and competence. A right view of God will supply them with a solid framework and roof of protection, enabling them to erect walls and windows that establish healthy boundaries and interaction with others. As God puts their house back in order, survivors can begin to select "new furniture"—habits, tastes, and ways of relating with others that more accurately reflect the person God created them to be.

BECOMING MYSELF

Furniture serves several functions. It provides comfort, pleases the senses, and expresses individuality. To survive the trauma of abuse, victims must often sacrifice their own comfort as they repress the truth about their abuse and the painful emotions that accompany it. They often ignore the development of their own unique tastes as they frantically fulfill the wishes and desires of others. Many victims stifle their individuality as they build walls to prevent further hurt.

Catrina, sexually abused by seven different men from childhood through college, has begun to recognize ways in which her abuse kept her true self hidden. "I survived by becoming a chameleon," she shared, "and carried over my people-pleasing mentality into all of my relationships. When I was with Chris, I became Chris. When I was with Peggy, I became Peggy. Now that I'm working through my recovery process, it scares me to discover that I'm not sure who the real 'me' is. My husband and I are remodeling our house, and I'm looking around for new furniture. But I've gone along with others' suggestions for so long, it's hard to get in touch with my own tastes. I'm not even sure what kind of furniture I like."

Out with the old, in with the new

1. *Comfortable habit patterns*. Survivors can replace their coping mechanisms of repressing the truth about their abuse and the painful emotions that accompanied it with "new furniture" suited to their comfort. New habits of "feeling their feelings" in the present will help to heal scarred emotions from the past. When they share with God and trusted friends the truth about their abuse and its effects, they will re-connect with their childlike spontaneity, enabling them to pursue new directions for their lives.

2. *Pleasing others*. As survivors pursue God's goals for their lives, they will develop a taste for adventure that can replace their fears of failure. "Old furniture" of fulfilling

others' desires and wishes at the expense of developing their own tastes may take on various forms. Adults abused as children may neglect their own needs and feel overly responsible for the needs of others. An unhealthy people-pleasing mentality could also show up in perfectionist drives that skew priorities and create workaholics, or in habits of avoiding confrontation by communicating wants and needs through a third party.

Those who fill their homes with "people-pleasing furniture" need to compare their life goals with God's goals for their lives. They must also challenge their fear of failure and make some decisions on their own, letting others take responsibility for their decisions and actions without needing to "fix" everyone.

3. *Individuality in relationships.* To select "new furniture" that expresses individuality is to develop healthy ways of relating that keeps one accessible to others. Because their trust was violated as children, abuse victims have difficulty trusting others. They often appear strong and in control but find it difficult to develop intimate friendships. This leads to denial and dishonesty in their relationships with others and within themselves. Abuse victims who build walls may point out faults in others that they fail to recognize in themselves. They often appear judgmental, over-critical, and self-righteous. Ultimately, their inability to control people and situations results in negative attitudes. Only as they allow God to melt their defenses and surrender their need for control to a God beyond their control will they experience the freedom to develop healthy relationships with others.

ABUSE HIDES OUR TRUE SELVES

Abuse affects a person emotionally in the same way that amblyopia, or a "lazy eye," affects a person physically.

Randy Carlson shared how he and his wife discovered that their daughter had amblyopia during a routine eye exam. "Both eyes were not aligned properly," Randy explained, "and one had started to shut off because the brain could not deal with conflicting messages."[1]

In the same way, experiencing abuse at the hands of a parent or a trusted caretaker presents a child with conflicting messages, causing the child to shut down.

Alice Miller, in *For Your Own Good*, contrasts the plight of abused children with that of concentration camp survivors. Former camp inmates will not doubt the tragic nature of their experiences because they went through the experience with others. Miller explains that the camp victim ". . . will never attempt to convince himself that the cruelty he was subjected to was for his own good or interpret the absurdity of the camp as a necessary pedagogical measure; he will usually not attempt to empathize with the motives of his persecutors. He will find people who have had similar experiences and share with them his feelings of outrage, hatred, and despair over the cruelty he has suffered."[2]

Unlike adults from concentration camps, abused children have no one with whom they can share their suffering. Instead, their brains shut off the conflicting messages of experiencing abuse at the hands of people entrusted to care for them by developing coping strategies. These coping skills enable children to survive the trauma of abuse. As God re-parents them, however, they need to let these patterns fall by the wayside.

THE CHILD WITHIN US

Jesus said, "I tell you the truth, anyone who will not receive the kingdom of God like a little child will never enter it" (Mark 10:15). Receiving God's kingdom like a little child means to reach out eagerly for all he has for us and to receive his blessings heartily and readily. Children naturally reach out for gifts with exuberant enthusiasm— unless acts of emotional, physical, or sexual abuse make them suspicious of kindness.

Christian psychologist Dr. Kevin Leman states, "The little boy or girl you once were, you still are."[3] What happened to us in the past affects the way we respond to events in the present. Statistics show that parents abused as children are six times more likely to abuse their own children.[4] Seventy percent of all prostitutes and eighty percent of female drug addicts have had a history of severe sexual abuse as children.[5] Childhood abuse can make it difficult for us to get in touch with the innocent, vulnerable child we once were.

A distinction must be drawn between "childish" and "childlike." Paul states in 2 Corinthians 13:11 that when he became a man he put away childish ways. The word used here for childish means an immature, simple-minded person. The childlike nature Jesus calls us to in Mark 10:15 refers to a stage in our development when all seemed fresh and new to us.

Months before the memories of my abusive incidents surface, I learned something about my past that surprised me. My mother mentioned how, at age five, I would happily dance down the sidewalk as I helped my father put insurance advertisements on people's doorknobs. I had no memories of myself as that child. The only child I remembered never spoke out of turn in the classroom, turned shyly away from strangers, and feared walking home alone.

I wondered why I couldn't remember myself as a happy, carefree little girl. A few weeks later I attended a workshop on codependency. The instructor asked us to close our eyes and picture ourselves sitting comfortably in a chair, looking out on our favorite scenery.

"Now imagine a little girl opening the door to your room," the instructor said. "She quietly moves over to your chair, whispers something in your ear, and then quietly walks out again."

At the conclusion of the exercise, I wept uncontrollably. My little girl had said, "I have so many dreams and so much energy. I love life!" I had lost touch with that part of myself.

A few months later God brought to my memory the abusive incidents that had damaged the exuberance and spontaneity of my "little girl." Slowly, he is helping me incorporate that lost part of me into my adult personality, showing me what it means to become like a little child so I can enter into the fullness of his kingdom.

When survivors begin to recognize the ways in which their abuse has kept their true self hidden and begin to replace their worn out coping mechanisms with "new furniture," they will begin to re-connect themselves with the childlike nature they had before they experienced the abuse. They can then reach out for God's nurturing and receive all he has for them.

TIME TO CONSIDER

1. What steps can survivors take to replace habit patterns of repressing the truth about their abuse and the painful emotions that accompany it?

2. What can they do to stop feeling overly responsible for the wants and needs of others?

3. What attitudes or actions characterize those who build walls of inaccessibility? How can they break down these walls?

4. Can you recall specific incidents when, as a child, you felt uninhibited and in love with life?

5. What does it mean to receive God's kingdom like a little child?

6. What pieces of "old furniture" do you need to get rid of? What steps will you take to select "new furniture"?

GOD'S NURTURING WORDS TO YOU

"When people brought their little children to me, asking that I touch and bless them, my disciples rebuked the people. My disciples thought I had more important things to do than to touch little children. How wrong they were! 'Anyone who does not receive the kingdom of God like a little child will never enter it,' I told them. I took those children into my arms, put my hands on them, and blessed them.

"Are you like my disciples, trying to distance that childlike part of yourself from me? Do not be afraid of me. I long to have you climb up into my arms. Feel them enfold you as you embrace my love. Receive all that I have for you." (Paraphrased from Mark 10:15.)

10

...

Growing in Wholeness

"Therefore, if anyone is in Christ, he is a new creation; the old has gone, the new has come!" (2 Cor. 5:17). Creation as used in this passage means "a founding of a city, colonization of a habitable place."[1] The moment we trust Christ to cleanse us from our sins, he takes up residence in our lives through his Holy Spirit. Our "colonization," however, is a process. Second Corinthians 3:18 explains, "And we, who with unveiled faces all reflect the Lord's glory, *are being transformed* into his likeness with ever-increasing glory, which comes from the Lord, who is the Spirit" (italics added). As we recover from the effects of childhood abuse we become more of the person God created us to be. Recovery is a process, and we are all unique people with whom God works individually. So, rather than outline specific steps survivors can take as they move toward wholeness, this chapter will discuss "recovery phrases."

"TRIGGERS AND TRACING" AND "FEEL TO HEAL"

Present situations often trigger unresolved issues from the past. Abuse victims may respond to an event with more emotion than it warrants when it touches on a volatile issue they never resolved in their past, such as feeling worthless or abandoned.

Those filled with the Holy Spirit can draw upon his power to recognize these overreactions. As a counselor and comforter, the Holy Spirit can help them trace the trigger to its unresolved origin and walk with them through the healing process.

Because I had suppressed my emotions for so long, it was hard to "feel my feelings" as I worked on my abuse issues. Events would trigger emotional responses, but I didn't know how to let my feelings surface long enough so that I could deal with them in a healthy way. Instead, I'd often crawl into bed at night, unable to sleep because of the fiery pain in my joints and throbbing head. As Alice Miller stated, "The truth about our childhood is stored up in our body, and although we can repress it, . . . someday the body will present its bill."[2]

My body presented its bill to me one night after I had excitedly told my parents about a new home my husband and I planned to purchase.

"Okay, Lord," I restlessly prayed in bed, "why is my body going whacky again? I had a great day!" I reviewed my conversation with my parents and tried to remember how I felt. I recalled that when I excitedly showed my mom samples of the tiles we had chosen for our new bathrooms, she hadn't shared my enthusiasm. My parents thought our purchase was a wise decision, but they couldn't share in our joy because they had recently sold their large home and moved into a small condominium. All of their profit went into their business.

Mom wiped a tear from under her glasses. "I've worked so hard for sixty years, and what do I have to show for it?"

As I re-played the scene in my mind, I remembered my parents' reactions had made my stomach tighten and left me feeling helpless. I slipped out of bed, moved to the front room couch, and asked God to help me process my feelings over that event.

After I put myself in God's presence and gave him permission to move through my life as he wished, I cried. "I can't fix it," I said over and over through my tears. Feelings tumbled over feelings, like water gushing over a dam. My therapist had once said, "You can't push a river, but you can get in an inner tube and float down it." I got into my "inner tube" and bounced down my emotional waterfall.

My journey stopped at a memory of myself at the age of six, playing records on the floor of our front room. Those records were my friends, and I loved their music. Then I remembered hearing a crack and feeling my stomach tighten as I realized I had sat on one of my records and broken it. I cried hard over that broken record. I had shown it to my mom, but she only said I needed to be more careful. I felt as if she had expected me to somehow fix the record. I saw myself as a little girl, trying to fit the sharp black pieces back together again like a puzzle.

As I sat on the couch now, a different kind of puzzle piece fit into place. I realized that I had emotionally responded to my parents' sadness that day by feeling responsible for their happiness. Emotionally, the little girl inside of me had screamed, "I can't fix it for you, Mom!"

When Love Is Not Perfect

My body was presenting its bill for all the times I had repressed my emotions when interpreting my parents' actions as requests for help that I couldn't provide.

God brought that old wound to the surface as he helped me understand an emotional trigger and trace its origin. Although I love my parents deeply, I'm not responsible to fix their problems.

Suddenly my two-year-old son woke up crying. As I entered Daniel's room, he pointed to the corner of his crib and cried, "Mommy fik, Mommy fik!" I picked Daniel up and cuddled him, trying to figure out what he wanted. Then I noticed that a corner knob on his crib had come off again. For some reason it had upset him. I pressed Daniel close to myself. "Yes, Mommy fix, Mommy fix." I found the piece, gave Daniel another hug, and then laid him down in his crib.

After crawling back into my own bed, I thanked the Lord for helping me to recognize a trigger and trace it back to an unresolved emotional issue from the past, that of taking responsibility for my parents' happiness. Because I allowed myself to feel the emotions surrounding this issue, God could heal by letting me see the truth. His nurturing in turn gave me the strength I needed to nurture Daniel.

If you respond to something with more emotion than the situation warrants, take a moment to ask yourself, "What was I feeling when that happened? Did I feel sad, angry, embarrassed, guilty, helpless, abandoned, afraid? Why did I feel that way? When else have I felt like that?" If you are successful in tracing an emotional trigger back to a point where you may have dammed up your feelings in order to protect yourself, ride your emotions through. Cry if you need to cry. Feel angry feelings without acting on them. As Paul said in Ephesians 4:26, "In your anger do not sin."

"Processing" your feelings is letting down emotional guards you may have put up since childhood in order to protect yourself from devastating hurt. Process your feelings by asking yourself, "What emotion am I feeling? How does that emotion make my body feel? Does my throat tighten? Does my stomach twinge?" If you are confused, "feel" the confusion. Let it run its course. You may want to stop the process once you get in touch with fears you've repressed since childhood. Fear puts you in touch with feeling abandoned—one of the scariest emotions for a child. When you "feel to heal," however, you will open up the deepest parts of yourself to God, allowing the healing balm of his Spirit to cleanse your wounds.

"HONOR YOUR PROCESS"

Honoring your process is another important recovery phrase. It means giving yourself time to recover from the effects of your abuse rather than expecting an overnight transformation.

After Eileen confronted her parents with the memories of her father and brother sexually abusing her, more than a year passed before she felt comfortable spending holidays with them again. "A few months after I told my parents about the childhood abuse," Eileen said, "we spent Christmas together. I immediately realized that I needed more time away from them to work through my recovery process.

"My dad watched television while my husband and brother-in-law talked. Dad said to no one in particular, 'It sure would be nice if we could hear this program.' Immediately, I fell into our old family pattern of triangled communication. I knew my dad's comment meant he wanted my husband and brother-in-law to stop talking, so I asked my husband to be quiet. Afterwards I felt angry at myself for falling into the same 'rescuer' trap for my dad, enabling him to avoid one-on-one confrontations. Then I remembered the phrase 'honor your process.' That helped me relax. It would take time for me to change old habits. It also gave me the courage to turn down invitations to family gatherings until I felt comfortable with my progress."

The Psalms illustrate "honor your process" ideas. In Psalm 3:1-3 King David wrote,

"O LORD, how many are my foes!
How many rise up against me!
Many are saying of me,
'God will not deliver him.' *Selah*
But you are a shield around me, O LORD;
you bestow glory on me and lift up my head."

The Hebrew word *selah* is a musical pause, interlude, or crescendo. David often inserted these musical pauses when he was moving from emotions such as fear or anger to an attitude of trust in God.

The heading for Psalm 3 says that David wrote this when he fled from his son Absalom. Absalom had won the hearts of the Israelites, causing David and his men to flee the capital. As they fled, a man from the tribe of Benjamin pelted David and his officials with stones. "Get out, get out, you man of blood, you scoundrel!" the Benjamite shouted. "The LORD has repaid you for all the blood you shed in the household of Saul, in whose place you have reigned. The LORD has handed the kingdom over to your son Absalom. You have come to ruin because you are a man of blood" (2 Sam. 16:7, 8).

In Psalm 3 David "felt his feelings." "How many rise up against me! Many are saying of me, 'God will not deliver him.' *Selah*." I believe David's *selah*s gave him time to "honor his process." He didn't wallow in his fear or anger, but neither did he regard those emotions as evidence of a

116

lack of faith. He grappled with his humanness, paused, and then looked to God to find refuge. "But you are a shield around me, O LORD."

Those abused as children will progress in their growth toward wholeness as they process their emotions. This will happen as they recognize emotional "triggers," tracing them to unresolved issues from the past. As they "feel to heal," they "honor their process," giving themselves the necessary time to develop new habit patterns.

"PROGRESS NOT PERFECTION"

A final recovery phrase that I find especially helpful is "progress not perfection." During the early stages of my recovery, I was easily angered or upset. If my children misbehaved and I reacted by yelling, I felt like a failure. At those times, however, the Lord would graciously remind me about "progress not perfection." That helped me to relax and make things right, which usually included apologizing to my kids, and move on.

Having added to our homes the new furniture of these recovery phrases, we can then open our front door and shake out the welcome mat.

TIME TO CONSIDER

1. According to the following verses, what is the role of the Holy Spirit in our recovery process? John 14:26; 15:26; 16:13, 14; Romans 8:11-17; 2 Corinthians 3:18.

2. What does the phrase "triggers and tracing" mean to you?

3. What does it mean to "feel to heal"? What are the benefits of processing our feelings?

4. What does it mean to "honor your process"?

5. Read 2 Samuel 16:1-14 and Psalm 4. Note the locations of the *selahs* in Psalm 4. If David wrote Psalm 4 under the same circumstances as Psalm 3, which was shortly after experiencing the events in 2 Samuel 16, what were some of his emotions? What could have made him feel this way? What did he do with those emotions? What was the result?

6. Have you been able to apply any of the recovery phrases this week? What was the result?

GOD'S NURTURING WORDS TO YOU

"Let me go with you through the valley of tears. Don't be afraid of your feelings. Those who sow in tears will reap the songs of joy. He who goes out weeping, carrying seed to sow, will return with songs of joy, carrying sheaves with him.

"A day will come when the old order of things will pass away. I will wipe every tear from your eyes. There will be no more death or mourning or crying or pain. In this world, however, you will have tribulation. That is why I sent my Spirit to live within you. Look to him as your counselor and comforter. My Spirit does not make you a slave to fear. You have received the Spirit of adoption. By him you can cry out '*Abba*, Father.' " (Paraphrased from Psalm 126:5, 6; Revelation 21:4; John 16:33; 14:16; Romans 8:15.)

Part VI

Shaking out the Welcome Mat

11

...

Forgive and Forget?

Can abuse survivors really forgive and forget? Valerie's father sexually abused her for more than ten years. "For many years I shook my fists at God and vowed, 'I will *never* forgive my dad,' " Valerie said. " 'It will never be all right that he did these things to me!' " Recently, however, Valerie realized that forgiving her father didn't mean she was excusing the abuse. "I began to see that God knew plenty about suffering, about abuse, and about being vulnerable," Valerie explained. "I began to see that God *is* good, and that child abuse, especially sexual abuse, is an abomination to him."

Although Valerie will never forget the abuse she suffered from her father, God enabled her to forgive him. "I experienced much healing and release in the act of forgiving my dad," she said.

FORGIVE AND FORGET—
WHAT DOES IT MEAN?

Forgiveness costs. God forgave our sins but at the expense of his son's life. To forgive someone means we allow ourselves to feel the pain of another's hurtful actions toward us, and yet release them from the debt they owe us for the damage they inflicted. We can only extend this kind of forgiveness if we have been released from our debts. Pastor and counselor David Seamands uses Jesus' parable of the unmerciful servant to illustrate this point.

A servant owed his master more than he could ever hope to repay. When the master demanded payment, the servant asked for an extension of time.

" 'Be patient with me,' he begged, 'and I will pay back everything.' The servant's master took pity on him, canceled the debt and let him go. But when that servant went out, he found one of his fellow servants who owed him a hundred denarii. He grabbed him and began to choke him. 'Pay back what you owe me!' he demanded" (Matt. 18:26-29).

Seamands explains that the servant didn't understand the mercy his master had extended to him. The master had canceled the servant's debt, even though the servant had only asked for more time to pay the money back. The servant thought he still owed his master the money, so he tried to collect on all the debts others owed him.[1]

When we truly understand that Christ has paid for our sins, we can freely release others from their debts to us. As Valerie discovered, however, that doesn't mean God asks us to excuse the hurt we've experienced. Quite the opposite. Only when we've felt the impact of another's hurt can we truly forgive their offense.

Philippians 3:10, 11, 13 says, "I want to know Christ

and the power of his resurrection and the fellowship of sharing in his sufferings, becoming like him in his death, and so, somehow, to attain to the resurrection from the dead. . . . But one thing I do: Forgetting what is behind and straining toward what is ahead, I press on toward the goal to win the prize for which God has called me heavenward in Christ Jesus."

According to *Strong's Concordance*, the word used here for "forget" means to "lose out of the mind."[2] When it comes to painful memories, we can't really "lose out of our mind" the abuse we suffered if its memory is locked in our emotions. To know the power of Jesus' resurrection and the fellowship of his sufferings, we must become like him in his death in whatever area keeps us from experiencing his nurturing. For example, if we suffer from feelings of abandonment and can't fully trust God and others, we need to "feel the feelings" of abandonment, processing them instead of repressing them, even as Jesus felt abandoned on the cross (Mark 15:34).

We share in Jesus' sufferings when we let ourselves feel the painful emotions associated with the memories of our abuse that we have tried to avoid feeling all of our lives. As we take our hurts to the Lord, he conforms them to his death. The word used for "becoming" like Jesus in his death means an adjustment of parts, shape, nature, or form. Our pain takes on a redeeming nature as we share in the fellowship of Jesus' sufferings. The tense of the word translated "becoming" is in the present, passive voice, meaning God is performing a continuous action on our behalf.

The Greek text of Philippians 3:13 emphasizes the tandem action of forgetting what is behind and straining toward what is ahead. "But one thing I do, the things on one hand behind forgetting, the things on the other before stretching forward to. . . ."[3] We will experience the power of Jesus' resurrection as we let go of the past and reach forward to what lies ahead, stepping into the unknown and unfamiliar with childlike faith in God's nurturing love.

CONFRONTING ABUSERS

How does forgiving our abusers relate to confronting them? Must we forgive them before we confront them or does one preclude the other? How can we know if we've forgiven someone? Will we feel different? God deals with each of us in unique ways, but general principles can provide us with direction.

One important purpose for confronting abusers is to put the responsibility for the abuse in their lap. When memories of the sexual abuse I had experienced at the hands of relatives surfaced, the point came when I felt like I would explode if I didn't confront them. I knew enough about their background to help me understand what could have prompted their actions, but I needed to let them own the responsibility for it. When I met with my first abuser, I told him what I had remembered and how it had affected my life and attitudes toward him. As often happens with abusers, he said he had no memory of the event. Survivors of abuse must prepare themselves for this. If our purpose in confronting our abuser is to obtain a plea for forgiveness or an admission of guilt, then we are not yet ready to confront them. We must be far enough along in our recovery process that denial on the part of the abuser will not affect our resoluteness to put the responsibility for the abuse where it belongs.

If a confrontation with our abuser is to further our healing and possibly aid the abuser, we must have forgiven before we confront. John 8:32 says that as Jesus' disciples we will know the truth and the truth will set us free. As God brings to light the truth about our abuse, we will be free of its hold only if we can confront without malice. As illustrated in the parable of the unmerciful servant, a lack of forgiveness on our part will only tighten the chains of our prison. If Jesus has not yet put to death the sting of our painful memories, enabling us to forgive our abuser from the heart, it would be better to wait until we are further along in our process before we confront.

Confrontation, however, is not necessary for healing to occur. Valerie's father died before she could work through her abuse issues, but she was able to forgive him and grow in wholeness without a confrontation.

Forgiveness is a decision of our will, whether or not feelings accompany it. Carol, abused by an older brother for several years, knew she was ready to confront him when she could do it not for revenge, but for reconciliation. Carol's parents were dead, so she decided to tell one of her sisters and her eldest brother about the abuse first, before confronting the abuser. She then wrote a letter to him, outlining exactly what he had done to her, how she had hated it, and, for many years, had borne the consequences of anorexia and a lack of trust in others because of the abuse.

Carol's eldest brother personally delivered Carol's letter to the brother who had abused her. When her abuser read the letter he wept and, for several days, considered committing suicide. Carol's eldest brother encouraged his abusive brother to get into counseling. Only after her abuser began to respond to counseling did Carol agree to meet with him.

When Carol met with her abuser in his counselor's office, she once again outlined what he had done to her. Afterward her brother said, "The mind is a strange thing, Carol. I've known I did some bad things to you, but I couldn't remember any of the details like you did." He broke down and wept again.

"I then did something I hadn't planned on doing," Carol shared. "I got out of my chair, embraced him, and let him hold me. It was the first time I could do that with joy instead of fear, pain, and terror."

Through his tears Carol's brother told her, "My life has been like a smudged blackboard with those things written on it. Now my blackboard's empty. I know you and God have forgiven me, and we can build again from here."

Like Valerie and Carol, forgiving and putting the things of the past behind us, we can shake out our welcome mat and strain toward what lies ahead. This will happen as we "feel the feelings" of our abusive issues, letting Jesus conform them to his death. Because we have received his forgiveness for all of our wrongs and have "lost out of our mind" what lies behind, we can freely extend forgiveness to our abusers in Jesus' resurrection power. When we confront our abusers with the consequences of their behavior, we allow them to take full responsibility for their actions—whether or not they choose to own it. The truth will set us free.

TIME TO CONSIDER

1. What does it mean to forgive someone?

2. Read Matthew 18:21-35. What does this story teach about forgiveness?

3. If we forgive someone, does that mean we absolve them of all responsibility for the wrong they did?

4. How can the emotional pain we experience as a result of our abuse take on a redeeming nature?

5. What are some healthy reasons for confronting an

abuser? What are some unhealthy reasons?

6. How can we know if we're ready to confront an abuser?

7. How does John 8:32 relate to confronting an abuser?

GOD'S NURTURING WORDS TO YOU

"My child, as you rest in my nurturing love, get rid of all bitterness, rage, and anger, along with every form of malice. Be kind and compassionate to one another, forgiving each other, just as in Christ, I forgave you.

"Do not love with words or tongue, but with actions and in truth. Have nothing to do with the fruitless deeds of darkness, but rather expose them. It is not your job to convict others of sin, but merely to tell the truth. My Holy Spirit will convict the world of guilt in regard to sin and righteousness and judgment. Leave that job to him to accomplish in his timing. I came to set captives free, and I long to do that for you." (Paraphrased from Ephesians 4:31, 32; 1 John 3:18; Ephesians 5:11; John 16:8; Luke 4:18.)

12

...

Pressing On

"One of my friends was sexually abused as a child," a writer explained to Stuart and Jill Briscoe in their "Ask the Briscoes" column of the *Christian Herald* magazine. "She's going for counseling but seems stuck in the past. I want to be a good friend but also want to tell her everyone has problems and to start looking ahead instead of back. How do I say this tactfully?"

The Briscoes encouraged this friend to be gentle, understanding, positive, and above all, sensitive to the pain her abused friend was suffering. "Pray for her, her counselor, and yourself as her friend. Read about the problem and be patient; no quick solutions exist."[1]

As survivors work through their recovery process, they grow in wholeness. Their growth can have negative as well as positive effects on those around them. Some friends may shout, "Get on with your life!" Others may try to listen sympathetically, bewildered by the whole process. Still others, those who have gotten in touch with their own deep hurt, will listen compassionately, extend a helping hand or a shoulder to cry on when necessary, and pray supportively. We must honor our process as God re-parents us, spending time with those who will encourage us as we move toward becoming all God created us to be.

For a while, our circle of friends may change, grow large, or shrink. Some may need the support and understanding of a small, safe, and supportive group like a Twelve-Step Group, Adult Children of Alcoholics or an Incest Survivors' group. Later we'll find ourselves strong enough to be the person God created us to be in all of our associations.

As God heals us, we naturally want to share that healing with others in distress. Second Corinthians 1:3 says, "Praise be to the God and Father of our Lord Jesus Christ, the Father of compassion and the God of all comfort, who comforts us in all our troubles, so that we can comfort those in any trouble with the comfort we ourselves have received from God."

The New Testament contains more than eighty "one another" passages encouraging Christians to love each other in specific ways. Some of the actions Scripture encourages us to take include being devoted to, living in harmony with, accepting, instructing, having equal concern for, bearing with, forgiving, teaching and admonishing, praying for, confessing our sins to, and clothing ourselves with humility toward one another. While working on our abuse issues, our group of confidants should include Christians who can help fulfill these "one another" admonitions in our lives. As we grow, we can then, in turn, fulfill these roles in the lives of others.

BARNABAS

Barnabas is an early Christian who fulfilled the "one another" admonitions. Acts 4:36, 37 gives us our first glimpse of him.

"Joseph, a Levite from Cyprus, whom the apostles called Barnabas (which means Son of Encouragement), sold a field he owned and brought the money and put it at the apostles' feet."

Acts 9:26, 27 tells the story of how Barnabas presented the newly converted Paul to the apostles as a brother in the Lord when all the other disciples had drawn back from Paul, fearing his zealous persecution of Christians.

The first believers known as "Christians" were those in the church of Antioch under the leadership of Barnabas. Many came to the Lord through his ministry, prompting Barnabas to seek out Paul to bring him back to Antioch to help with the work there. The Antioch church later sent out Paul and Barnabas on their first missionary journey. Acts 13:13 tells us that John, also known as John Mark, a cousin of Barnabas, accompanied them on this journey as far as Perga in Pamphylia, where John returned to Jerusalem.

When Paul suggested that he and Barnabas embark on a second missionary journey to visit the brothers they had preached to on their first trip, Barnabas wanted to take John Mark with them.

"But Paul did not think it wise to take him, because he had deserted them in Pamphylia and had not continued with them in the work. They had such a sharp disagreement that they parted company. Barnabas took Mark and sailed for Cyprus, but Paul chose Silas and left, commended by the brothers to the grace of the Lord" (Acts 15:38-41).

Taken under his wing by the "Son of Encouragement," John Mark later went on to write the gospel of Mark.

When Love Is Not Perfect

When Paul was in prison he wrote to Timothy requesting, "Get Mark and bring him with you, because he is helpful to me in my ministry" (2 Tim. 4:11).

Barnabas shared his material goods with those in need. He admonished the early disciples to accept Paul as their brother. He preached to people in Antioch, bringing many to the Lord. Considering how to spur others on toward love and good deeds, Barnabas sought out Paul and brought him from Tarsus to help with the work in Antioch. With humility and love, Barnabas helped train a former "missionary deserter" who went on to write a gospel and to help Paul while he was in prison.

As we experience God's comfort through his Spirit, his Word, and his people, we can reach out and touch the lives of others with "the comfort we ourselves have received from God" (2 Cor. 1:3).

God may put people in our lives who are taking their first steps toward recovery. Our sensitivity, compassion, and friendship can help mirror God's love to them as God begins his re-parenting process in their lives.

We may also run into people who exhibit some of the characteristics of an adult abused as a child but who make no mention of it. By judiciously sharing our struggles, they may feel free enough to share their hurts. Those who have not experienced abuse themselves but wish to minister to abuse victims can share illustrations from those who are in recovery.

When we reach out to others as God directs, we, like living stones, will be built into a spiritual house, to declare the praises of him who called us out of darkness into his wonderful light (see 1 Peter 2:5, 9). As this household is built upon God's firm foundation, those of us dwelling in the house "will no longer be infants, tossed back and forth by the waves, and blown here and there by every wind of teaching and by the cunning and craftiness of men in their deceitful scheming. Instead, speaking the truth in love, we will in all things grow up into him who is the Head, that is, Christ. From him the whole body, joined and held together by every supporting ligament, grows and builds itself up in love, as each part does its work" (Eph. 4:14-16).

TIME TO CONSIDER

1. As God re-parents us, how can our growth have a positive effect on others? Negative effect?

2. Look up the following references. What actions do these "one another" passages admonish us to take? Romans 12:10, 16; 14:13; 15:7, 14; 1 Corinthians 12:25; Galatians 5:13; 6:2; Ephesians 4:1, 2, 32; 5:21; Colossians 3:13, 16; 1 Thessalonians 4:18; Hebrews 3:13; 10:24, 25; James 5:16; 1 Peter 1:22; 4:9; 5:5; 1 John 3:11; 4:11, 12.

3. Write down the "one another" actions you find easy to fulfill. Which ones do you find more difficult to carry out? Why?

4. Read Proverbs 3:27, 28 and 18:21. What do these passages say about encouragement?

5. Write a prayer to God expressing your commitment to encourage others with the comfort you have received from God.

GOD'S NURTURING WORDS TO YOU

"My child, continue to place your confidence in me. As you do, you will be like a tree planted by the water that sends out its roots by the stream. You will not fear when heat comes. Being rooted and established in my love, you will begin to grasp how wide and long and high and deep my love is for you, filling you up to the measure of all the fullness of God.

"In a large house there are articles not only of gold and silver, but also of wood and clay; some are for noble purposes and some for ignoble. As you grow in wholeness, you will be an instrument for noble purposes, made holy and useful to me, prepared to do any good work. You will rebuild ancient ruins and raise up age-old foundations. You will be called Repairer of Broken Walls and Restorer of Streets. You will find joy in me. I will cause you to ride on the heights of the land, feasting on the inheritance of your heavenly Father. Come. Enter into the work I have prepared for you." (Paraphrased from Jeremiah 17:7, 8; Ephesians 3:17-19; 2 Timothy 2:20, 21; Isaiah 58:12-14.)

Source Notes

INTRODUCTION

1. Kahlil Gibran, *The Prophet* (New York: Alfred A. Knopf, 1989), p. 32.

CHAPTER 1

1. "Manslaughter Verdict in Girl's Beating Death," *San Jose Mercury News*, January 31, 1989, p. 1A, 10A.

George Hackett with Peter McKillop and Dorothy Wang, "A Tale of Abuse," *Newsweek*, December 12, 1988, pp. 56-61.

2. John Crewdson, *By Silence Betrayed* (Boston: Little, Brown, and Company, 1988), p. 24.

3. Crewdson, p. 25.

4. Jean Seligman with Karen Springen, Jodi Steward, Deborah Witherspoon, and Laurean Lazarovici, "Emotional Child Abuse," *Newsweek*, October 3, 1988, p. 48.

5. Seligman, Springen, Stewart, Witherspoon, and Lazarovici, p. 48.

6. Carolyn Weaver, "Sally Cooper," *Ms. Magazine*, July/August, 1987, p. 112.

7. Seligman, Springen, Stewart, Witherspoon, and Lazarovici, p. 48.

8. "Girl's Beating Death Prompts FBI Probe," *The San Francisco Examiner*, November 9, 1988, p. A6.

   Frank Trippet, Alan Ota, and John Snell, "The Death of Dayna," *Time*, October 31, 1988, p. 19.

9. Margaret O. Hyde, *Sexual Abuse—Let's Talk About It* (Philadelphia: The Westminster Press, 1987), p. 15.

10. Hyde, pp. 15, 16.

11. Hyde, p. 16.

12. Crewdson, pp. 24, 28.

13. Kevin Leman and Randy Carlson, *Unlocking the Secrets of Your Childhood Memories* (Nashville: Thomas Nelson Publishers, 1989), p. 160.

CHAPTER 2

1. Weaver, p. 116.

2. Hyde, p. 28.

   Maria Roy, *Children in the Crossfire* (Deerfield Beach, FL: Health Communications, Inc., 1988), p. 60.

3. Stanislaus County Department of Mental Health, "General Indicators of Sexual Abuse," Children's Self-Help Project (Modesto, CA: 1988), p. 1.

4. Roy, p. 60.

5. "Facts About Children of Alcoholism, Kids Are Special" (San Jose, CA: 1989), p. 1.

6. Roy, p. 60.

7. John Bradshaw, *On the Family* (Deerfield Beach, FL: Health Communications, Inc., 1988), p. 123.

8. Hyde, p. 25.

9. Pamela Portwood, *Rebirth of Power* (Racine, WI: Mother Courage Press, 1987), p. vi.

10. Portwood, p. vi.

11. Bradshaw, p. 145.

12. Bradshaw, p. 158.

13. Bradshaw, p. 159.

14. Bradshaw, p. 160.

15. Robin Norwood, *Women Who Love Too Much* (New York: Pocket Books, 1985), pp. 65-67.

16. Roy, p. 15.

17. Hyde, p. 59.

18. Bradshaw, p. 137.

19. "Ombudsman of Child Abuse," *Ebony*, February, 1987, p. 82.

Roy, pp. 61, 62.

20. Alice Miller, *Thou Shalt Not Be Aware* (New York: Farrar, Straus, Giroux, 1984), p. 318.

21. David Seamands, *Putting Away Childish Things* (Wheaton, IL: Victor Books, 1988), p. 10.

CHAPTER 3

1. Barry Witt and Kristin Huckshorn, "2 Girls Slain; Father at Large," *San Jose Mercury News*, April 16, 1989, pp. 1A, 22A.

2. Norwood, pp. 14, 15.

3. Bradshaw, p. 77.

4. Michael Weissberg, *Dangerous Secrets* (New York: W.W. Norton & Co., 1983), p. 44.

5. Dorothy Corkille Briggs, *Your Child's Self-Esteem* (New York: Doubleday, 1970), pp. 3, 4.

6. Dr. Charles Whitfield, *Healing the Child Within* (Deerfield Beach, FL: Health Communications, Inc., 1989), p. 18.

7. Erik H. Erikson, IDENTITY Youth and Crisis (New York: W.W. Norton & Co., 1968), p. 96.

8. Spiros Zodhiates, *The Hebrew-Greek Key Study Bible, Lexical Aids to the Old Testament* (Chattanooga, TN: AMG Publishers, 1984), p. 1646.

9. Erikson, p. 127.

10. Daniel Chu, Bonnie Johnson, Lois Armstrong, Jennifer Ash, and Todd Gold, "Susan Sullivan," *People Weekly*, April 18, 1988, pp. 107, 108.

CHAPTER 4

1. Norwood, p. 23.

2. Meoldy Beattie, *Codependent No More* (New York: Harper/Hazelden), pp. 37-40.

3. Larry Crabb, *Inside Out* (Colorado Springs: NavPress, 1988), p. 184.

4. Charles Swindoll, *Dropping Your Guard* (Waco, TX: Word Books, 1983), p. 101.

CHAPTER 5

1. Paul Chance and Jonnae C. Ostrom, "The Trouble with Love," *Psychology Today*, February, 1988, p. 22.

2. Nathan J. Stone, *Names of God* (Chicago: Moody Bible Institute of Chicago, 1944), p. 27.

CHAPTER 7

1. Norwood, p. 21.

2. Zodhiates, pp. 1687, 1706.

CHAPTER 8

1. Norwood, p. 23.
2. Twelve-Step groups meet a variety of needs:
   - Alcoholics Anonymous (A.A.) helps those addicted to alcohol.
   - Al-Anon supports the family members and friends of alcoholics.
   - Overeaters Anonymous (O.A.) supports those whose eating is out of control.
   - Narcotics Anonymous (N.A.) helps drug abusers.

Ask your local library if they have a list of community services for your area, or check the phone book in the community services section to find a local Twelve-Step group that will meet your needs.

Parents United will send a listing of the areas in which Parents United, Daughters United, and Sons United meetings are held if you send a stamped self-addressed envelope to P.O. Box 952, San Jose, CA 95108. The Parents United groups are for those who have been the aggressor in an incestuous relationship, mothers of incest victims, or children and adults sexually abused by parents or other trusted adults or family members. The Child Protective Services or Department of Social Services may also have listings of these groups that meet in your area.

CHAPTER 9

1. Kevin Leman and Randy Carlson, *Unlocking the Secrets of Your Childhood Memories* (Nashville: Thomas Nelson Publishers, 1989), p. 160.
2. Alice Miller, *For Your Own Good* (New York: Farrar, Straus, Giroux, 1983), pp. 116, 117.
3. Leman and Carlson, p. 13.

4. Barbara Kantrowitz with Pat Wingert, Pataricia King, Kate Robbins, and Tessa Namuth, "And Thousands More," *Newsweek*, December 12, 1988, p. 59.

5. Miller, *Thou Shalt Not Be Aware*, p. 326.

CHAPTER 10

1. Zodhiates, p. 1705.
2. Miller, *Thou Shalt Not Be Aware*, p. 318.

CHAPTER 11

1. David Seamands, *Healing for Damaged Emotions* (Wheaton, IL: Victor Books, 1987), p. 30.

2. James Strong, *The Exhaustive Concordance of the Bible* (McLean, VA: MacDonald Publishing Co.), p. 31.

3. Alfred Marshall, *The Revised Standard Version Interlinear Greek-English New Testament* (Grand Rapids, MI: Zondervan Publishing House, 1958), p. 785.

CHAPTER 12

1. Stuart and Jill Briscoe, "Ask the Briscoes," *Christian Herald*, January, 1989, pp. 8-10.

Support Group Leader's Guide

Issue-oriented, problem-wrestling, life-confronting—Heart Issue books are appropriate for adult Sunday school classes, individual study, and especially for support groups. Here are guidelines to encourage and facilitate support groups.

SUPPORT GROUP GUIDELINES

The small group setting offers individuals the opportunity to commit themselves to personal growth through mutual caring and support. This is especially true of Christian support groups, where from five to twelve individuals meet on a regular basis with a mature leader to share their personal experiences and struggles over a specific "heart issue." In such a group, individuals develop trust and accountability with each other and the Lord.

Because a support group's purpose differs from a Bible study or prayer group, it needs its own format and guidelines.

Let's look at the ingredients of a support group:
- Purpose
- Leadership
- Meeting Format
- Group Guidelines

PURPOSE

The purpose of a Heart Issue support group is to provide:

1. An *opportunity* for participants to share openly and honestly their struggles and pain over a specific issue in a non-judgmental, Christ-centered framework.

2. A *"safe place"* where participants can gain perspective on a mutual problem and begin taking responsibility for their responses to their own situations.

3. An *atmosphere* that is compassionate, understanding, and committed to challenging participants from a biblical perspective.

Support groups are not counseling groups. Participants come to be supported, not fixed or changed. Yet, as genuine love and caring are exchanged, people begin to experience God's love and acceptance. As a result, change and healing take place.

The initiators of a support group need to be clear about its specific purpose. The following questions are examples of what to consider before starting a small group.

1. What type of group will this be? A personal growth group, a self-help group, or a group structured to focus on a certain theme? Is it long-term, short-term, or ongoing?

2. Who is the group for? A particular population? College students? Single women? Divorced people?

3. What are the goals for the group? What will members gain from it?

4. Who will lead or co-lead the group? What are his/her qualifications?

5. How many members should be in the group? Will new members be able to join the group once it is started?

6. What kind of structure or format will the group have?

7. What topics will be explored in the support book and to what degree will this be determined by the group members and to what degree by the leaders?

LEADERSHIP

Small group studies often rotate leadership among participants, but because support groups usually meet for a specific time period with a specific mutual issue, it works well to have one leader or a team of co-leaders responsible for the meetings.

Good leadership is essential for a healthy, balanced group. Qualifications include character and personality traits as well as life experience and, in some cases, professional experience.

Personal Leadership Characteristics
COURAGE

One of the most important traits of effective group leaders is courage. Courage is shown in willingness (1) to be open to self-disclosure, admitting their own mistakes and taking the same risks they expect others to take; (2) to confront another, and, in confronting, to understand that love is the goal; (3) to act on their beliefs and hunches; (4) to be emotionally touched by another and to draw on their experiences in order to identify with the other; (5) to continually examine their inner self; (6) to be direct and honest with members; and (7) to express to the group their

143

fears and expectations about the group process. (Leaders shouldn't use their role to protect themselves from honest and direct interaction with the rest of the group.)

WILLINGNESS TO MODEL

Through their behavior, and the attitudes conveyed by it, leaders can create a climate of openness, seriousness of purpose, acceptance of others, and the desirability of taking risks. Group leaders should have had some moderate victory in their own struggles, with adequate healing having taken place. They recognize their own woundedness and see themselves as persons in process as well. Group leaders lead largely by example—by doing what they expect members to do.

PRESENCE

Group leaders need to be emotionally present with the group members. This means being touched by others' pain, struggles, and joys. Leaders can become more emotionally involved with others by paying close attention to their own reactions and by permitting these reactions to become intense. Fully experiencing emotions gives leaders the ability to be compassionate and empathetic with their members. At the same time, group leaders understand their role as facilitators. They know they're not answer people; they don't take responsibility for change in others.

GOODWILL AND CARING

A sincere interest in the welfare of the others is essential in group leaders. Caring involves respecting, trusting, and valuing people. Not every member is easy to care for, but leaders should at least want to care. It is vital that leaders become aware of the kinds of people they care for easily and the kinds they find it difficult to care for. They can gain this awareness by openly exploring their reactions to members. Genuine caring must be demonstrated; merely saying so is not enough.

Some ways to express a caring attitude are: (1) inviting a person to participate but allowing that person to decide how far to go; (2) giving warmth, concern, and support when, and only when it is genuinely felt; (3) gently confronting the person when there are obvious discrepancies between a person's words and her behavior; and (4) encouraging people to be what they could be without their masks and shields. This kind of caring requires a commitment to love and a sensitivity to the Holy Spirit.

OPENNESS

To be effective, group leaders must be open with themselves, open to others in groups, open to new experiences, and open to life-styles and values that differ from their own. Openness is an attitude. It doesn't mean that leaders reveal every aspect of their personal lives; it means that they reveal enough of themselves to give the participants a sense of person.

Leader openness tends to foster a spirit of openness within the group; it permits members to become more open about their feelings and beliefs; and it lends a certain fluidity to the group process. Self-revelation should not be manipulated as a technique. However, self-evaluation is best done spontaneously, when appropriate.

NONDEFENSIVENESS

Dealing frankly with criticism is related closely to openness. If group leaders are easily threatened, insecure in their work of leading, overly sensitive to negative feedback, and depend highly on group approval, they will probably encounter major problems in trying to carry out their leadership role. Members sometimes accuse leaders of not caring enough, of being selective in their caring, of structuring the sessions too much, of not providing enough direction, of being too harsh. Some criticism may be fair, some unfair. The crucial thing for leaders is to nondefensively explore with their groups the feelings that are legitimately produced by the leaders and those that represent what is upsetting the member.

STRONG SENSE OF SELF

A strong sense of self (or personal power) is an important quality of leaders. This doesn't mean that leaders would manipulate or dominate; it means that leaders are confident of who they are and what they are about. Groups "catch" this and feel the leaders know what they are doing. Leaders who have a strong sense of self recognize their weaknesses and don't expend energy concealing them from others. Their vulnerability becomes their strength as leaders. Such leaders can accept credit where it's due, and at the same time encourage members to accept credit for their own growth.

STAMINA

Group leading can be taxing and draining as well as exciting and energizing. Leaders need physical and emotional stamina and the ability to withstand pressure in order to remain vitalized until the group sessions end. If leaders give in to fatigue when the group bogs down, becomes resistive, or when members drop out, the effectiveness of the whole group could suffer. Leaders must be aware of their own energy level, have outside sources of spiritual and emotional nourishment, and have realistic expectations for the group's progress.

SENSE OF HUMOR

The leaders who enjoy humor and can incorporate it appropriately into the group will bring a valuable asset to the meetings. Sometimes humor surfaces as an escape from healthy confrontations and sensitive leaders need to identify and help the group avoid this diversion. But because we often take ourselves and our problems so seriously, we need the release of humor to bring balance and perspective. This is particularly true after sustained periods of dealing seriously with intensive problems.

CREATIVITY

The capacity to be spontaneously creative, to approach each group session with fresh ideas is a most important characteristic for group leaders. Leaders who are good at discovering new ways of approaching a group and who are willing to suspend the use of established techniques are unlikely to grow stale. Working with interesting co-leaders is another way for leaders to acquire fresh ideas.

GROUP LEADERSHIP SKILLS

Although personality characteristics of the group leader are extremely significant, by themselves they do not ensure a healthy group. Leadership skills are also essential. The following need to be expressed in a sensitive and timely way:

ACTIVE LISTENING

Leaders need to absorb content, note gestures, observe subtle changes in voice or expression, and sense underlying messages. For example, a woman may be talking about her warm and loving feelings toward her husband, yet her body may be rigid and her fists clenched.

EMPATHY

This requires sensing the subjective world of the participant. Group leaders, in addition to being caring and open, must learn to grasp another's experience and at the same time maintain their separateness.

RESPECT AND POSITIVE REGARD

In giving support, leaders need to draw on the positive assets of the members. Where differences occur, there needs to be open and honest appreciation and toleration.

WARMTH

Smiling has been shown to be especially important in the

communication of warmth. Other nonverbal means are: voice tone, posture, body language, and facial expression.
GENUINENESS

Leaders need to be real, to be themselves in relating with others, to be authentic and spontaneous.

FORMAT

The format of meetings will differ vastly from group to group, but the following are generally accepted as working well with support groups.
MEETING PLACE

This should be a comfortable, warm atmosphere. Participants need to feel welcome and that they've come to a "safe place" where they won't be overheard or easily distracted. Some groups will want to provide baby-sitting.
OPENING

Welcome participants. The leader should introduce herself and the members should also introduce themselves. It is wise to go over the "ground rules" at every meeting and especially at first or when there are newcomers. Some of these would include:

1. Respect others' sharing by keeping what is said in the group confidential.

2. Never belittle the beliefs or expressions of another.

3. Respect the time schedule. Try to arrive on time and be prompt in leaving.

4. Feel free to contact the leader at another time if there are questions or need for additional help.

Many meetings open with a brief time of prayer and worship and conclude with prayer. It often helps to ask for informal prayer requests and brief sharing so that the group begins in a spirit of openness.
MEETING

Leaders can initiate the meeting by focusing on a

particular issue (or chapter if the group is studying a book). It is wise to define the focus of the specific meeting so that the group can stay on track for the entire session. (See Group Guidelines below.)

CLOSING

Strive for promptness without being abrupt. Give opportunity for those who need additional help to make an appointment with the leader. Be alert to any needing special affirmation or encouragement as they leave.

GROUP GUIDELINES

Because this is a support group, not an advice group, the leader will need to establish the atmosphere and show by her style how to relate lovingly and helpfully within the group. Participants need to know the guidelines for being a member of the group. It is a wise practice to repeat these guidelines at each meeting and especially when newcomers attend. The following guidelines have proven to be helpful to share with support groups:

1. You have come to give and receive support. No "fixing." We are to listen, support, and be supported by one another—not give advice.

2. Let other members talk. Please let them finish without interruption.

3. Try to step over any fear of sharing in the group. Yet do not monopolize the group's time.

4. Be interested in what someone else is sharing. Listen with your heart. Never converse privately with someone else while another member is addressing the group.

5. Be committed to express your feelings from the heart. Encourage others to do the same. It's all right to feel angry, to laugh, or to cry.

6. Help others own their feelings and take responsibility for change in their lives. Don't jump in with an easy

answer or a story on how you conquered their problem. Relate to where they are.

7. Avoid accusing or blaming. Speak in the "I" mode about how something or someone made *you* feel. Example: "I felt angry when. . . ."

8. Avoid ill-timed humor to lighten emotionally charged times. Let participants work through their sharing even if it is hard.

9. Keep names and sharing of other group members confidential.

10. Because we are all in various stages of growth, please give newcomers permission to be new and old-timers permission to be further along in their growth. This is a "safe place" for all to grow and share their lives.

Appendix A

As mentioned in Chapter 10, recovering from abuse is a process, and this book has emphasized recovery phrases and models rather than outlining specific steps. However, below is a chart group leaders have found helpful in identifying where abuse survivors are in their recovery process. For example, if someone seems to have trouble choosing healthy ways to get their needs met, perhaps they still haven't identified some of the *unhealthy* ways they try to meet their needs. If they have trouble "feeling their feelings," perhaps you could suggest a time to meet with them personally when you could help them work through level one, admitting their abuse to you, one-on-one, which may help them feel safer than sharing about their abuse in the larger group. Keep in mind that abuse survivors will cycle through these levels many times during their recovery process. Each time, however, they will cycle through at a greater level of maturity. Abuse survivors will also experience low periods when they feel like they are making no progress, or are retreating backwards. Assure them that this is a normal part of the growth process and encourage them simply to continue taking a step at a time.

LEVELS OF RECOVERY

Develop a Plan for Reaching out to Others

Choose Healthy Ways to Get Needs Met

Identify Ways We Try to Meet Needs
That Aren't Healthy

Recognize Needs That Weren't Met

Feel the Feelings

Admit/Share the Abuse